CW00740567

ELIZABETH TAYLOR

A Life in Pictures

First published in Great Britain in 2008 by Pavilion Books
An imprint of Anova Books Company Ltd
10 Southcombe Street, London W14 0RA

First published in France in 2008 by YB Editions
Biography © Alexander Thiltges, 2008
Other text © Yann-Brice Dherbier, 2008
Cover photography © MPTV
Layout © Renaud Sauteret (sauteret@free.fr)
Editor (UK): Kate Burkhalter
Translation: JMS Publishing

ISBN : 978-1-86205-832-3
Reproduction: Ateliers du Regard
Printed and bound by EBS, Italy
10 9 8 7 6 5 4 3 2 1

www.anovabooks.com

ELIZABETH TAYLOR

A Life in Pictures

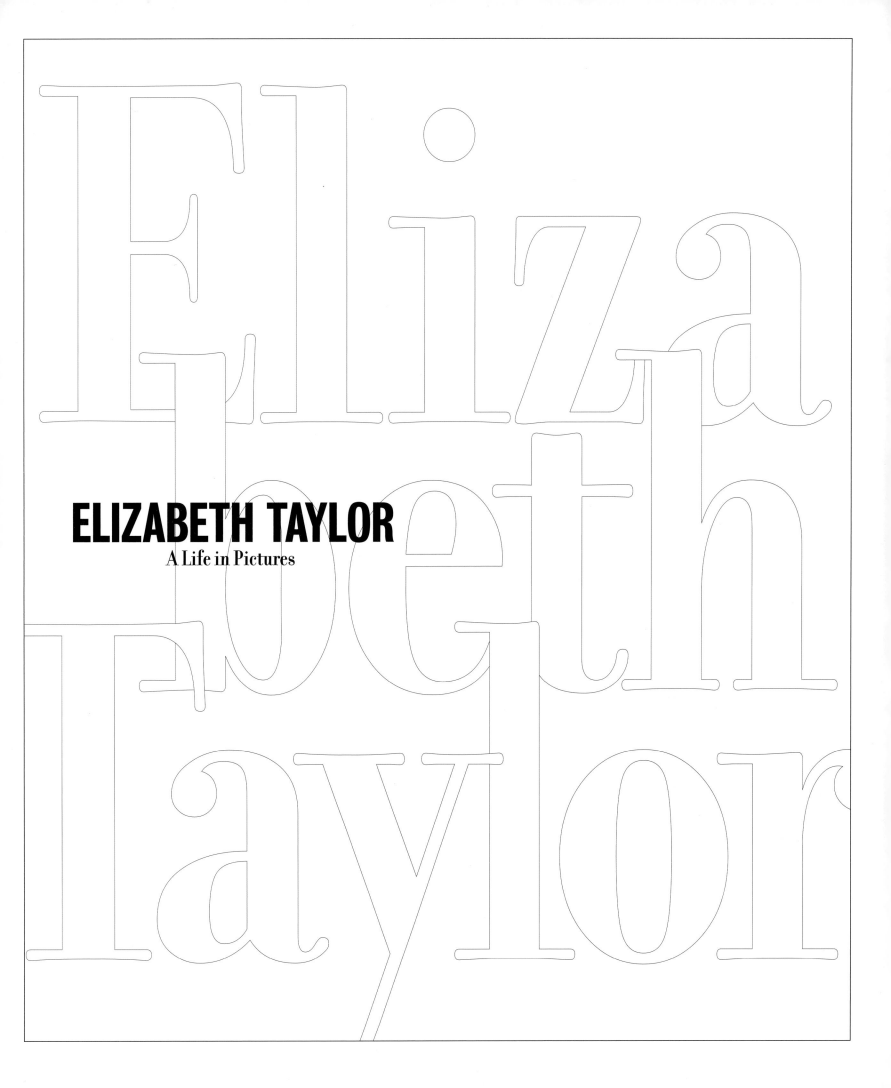

ELIZABETH TAYLOR

What do we know about the woman described as the 'sacred monster' or the 'diva' of Hollywood? For a start, some snippets about the caprices of a star: Elizabeth Taylor is late for everything (she generally makes people wait for two to five hours), hates being called 'Liz' ('my real friends just call me "Elizabeth"'), adores animals (she lives with a string of cats, dogs and other pets that mess on the carpets and claw her expensive evening dresses). We also know that she is noted in Hollywood for her irreverent and often obscene language. We know about her collection of diamonds and of husbands. But, clichés apart, who *is* Elizabeth Taylor?

Although she began her career playing the archetypal sweet, gentle child-woman, the actress quickly became identified with 1950s consumerism, then with pop culture and counter-culture before metamorphosing into an icon of sexuality and excess. At once conformist and rebellious, charming yet sour-tempered, submissive to male fantasies yet an independent woman, both retrograde and feminist, a product of her time yet fundamentally outside of it, Elizabeth Taylor embodies a host of contradictions that make her difficult to define.

In 1993 she summed up her life to a journalist from *People* magazine: 'Everything was handed to me – looks, fame, wealth, honour, love. I rarely had to fight for anything. But I've paid for that luck with disasters – the deaths of so many good friends, terrible illnesses, destructive addictions, broken marriages. All things considered, I'm damned lucky to be still alive!' [Spoto] Certainly, although the beginning of her career did not seem to indicate troubles ahead, Elizabeth Taylor's life has been far from rosy, but as she herself says, 'I'm a survivor – a living example of what people can go through and survive.' [Spoto]

When she was born on 27 February 1932 Elizabeth was not at all the little princess that her parents had looked forward to; her features were large, she was covered in downy fuzz and no one could have suspected that a few years later she would become an icon of feminine beauty worldwide. Her mother Sara said of her infant, 'Her hair was long and black. Her ears were covered with thick black fuzz and inlaid into the sides of her head; her nose looked like a tip-tilted button and her tiny face was so tightly closed it looked as if it would never unfold.' [Spoto]

Just as in a fairytale, this ugliness quickly turned into the most radiant beauty. From a very early age Elizabeth dazzled everyone who came into contact with her; they couldn't help falling under the charm of her bewitching eyes, which were a deep violet-blue, set off by long dark eyelashes. Her blue-black curly hair and the beauty spot on her cheek contrasted with her delicate porcelain complexion.

Elizabeth Rosemond Taylor was born in Hampstead, a wealthy and leafy residential area of London. Her American parents had decided to move to Europe in 1927 and she spent the first seven years of her life in the English capital, surrounded by nannies, chauffeurs and riding-instructors.

The childhood of the little princess

Elizabeth Taylor's story really began, however, in a peaceful little town in the south of Kansas where people talk with a piercing accent. Her parents met in Arkansas City while World War 1 raged in Europe. Sara Warmbrodt was a beautiful young woman, full of spirit and life, and the reserved and rather naïve Francis Taylor immediately fell in love with her. The two adolescents, desperately bored in their little township, dreamed of an exciting life far from America's heartland. Sara aspired to become a world-famous actress and her mother, who was a talented amateur singer and pianist, did nothing to discourage her. The life story of Elizabeth Taylor is clearly influenced by a long line of determined, intrepid and enterprising women; in this family, it was the mother who dominated and made the decisions, for better or worse. The future actress's first name was that of both her grandmothers, as if to link her firmly into this great matriarchal line.

When the war ended, Francis , now 21, was taken on as an apprentice to his uncle Howard Young, an art dealer in St. Louis. The young man seemed made for this profession – to the extent that Howard placed confidence in his nephew and decided to open a new gallery in New York with him. They specialized in European painting of the 18th and 19th centuries and the gallery quickly became successful. It was now 1919 and the brink of the Roaring 20s and the Jazz Age; money flowed like water and New York's nouveaux riches splashed out on these artistic masterpieces.

Meanwhile Sara had also left her small Midwestern home to study drama in Kansas City. She would not meet Francis again for several years, and then only by pure chance.

Sara's overriding ambition was to be known, famous and, if possible, celebrated. Finding her surname common she took Sara Sothern as her stage name and worked hard at meeting influential actors who might help her career. She began with a series of minor roles in small provincial companies, landing her first important part in *The Fool*, which opened at Los Angeles' Majestic Theatre in 1922. It was panned by the critics but the producers were determined to bring it to New York.

Although Sara wanted to stay in California, hoping to break into the movies, she was persuaded to stay with the production when it opened on Broadway, where it was somewhat better received and her acting was praised. A contract was signed to take the play to London, where it ran for five months at the Apollo Theatre. Again, Sara was thrilled by her success; the public clamoured for bits of her dress and locks of her hair and the Princess Royal came to her dressing room to present her with a diamond brooch. This passion for presents, notably precious stones, was one she would transmit to Elizabeth. Sara would later relive success and public adulation through her daughter, on whom she projected all her unachieved hopes.

Although Sara acted in other plays that were more or less well received by the critics and the public, her career never really took off and once she returned to New York she never regained the success she had enjoyed in England. In 1926 she was reunited with her old flame, Francis Taylor, following a chance meeting in a New York nightclub. Francis had acquired good taste and elegance and his business was doing well, which pleased the pretty actress whom he courted assiduously, sending her a daily bouquet of roses and inviting her to dinner. When he told her that his uncle wanted him to manage a new gallery in London, Sara accepted his proposal. They were married at the end of 1926 and Sara retired from the stage in early 1927.

While this was an agonizing decision for her, she was nevertheless pleased to be living in style, with plenty of refinement, luxury and visits to the great European capitals. Initially the couple lived in an apartment at the prestigious Carlton Hotel but towards the end of 1928, when Sara found she was expecting her first child, the young couple leased a two-bedroom house with a garden overlooking Hampstead Heath. Their first child, Howard, was born in June 1929. A beautiful baby with blue eyes and golden curls, 'from the first, he looked like a Botticelli angel', said his mother. Unfortunately, the same could not be said of his sister Elizabeth. born four years later.

The Taylor family were unaffected by the economic Depression and lived in carefree luxury with a nanny, cook and chauffeur. Soon they needed more room and moved a short distance away, paying cash for a large house with a tennis-court, again overlooking Hampstead Heath. This was the world into which a sturdy baby with unprepossessing features was born – and named Elizabeth Taylor.

At birth, the princess for whom her mother had waited so long was covered with a soft down of black hair, but this fuzz soon disappeared and Elizabeth's magnificent lavender-blue eyes gave her a disturbing, almost bewitching look. Elizabeth had a pretty little face, luminous eyes, long eyelashes and beautiful dark hair. Her porcelain-doll complexion was set off by a small, charming mole on her right cheek, which even in childhood her mother accentuated with a touch of black pencil. Above all, the mischievous child knew how to capture adult attention, a talent that would prove crucial to her career as an infant prodigy in the cinema. Even as a two-year-old, Sara encouraged her daughter to have the manners of a great lady. It should have been enough for Elizabeth to be a model young girl but her mother was moulding her, preparing Elizabeth for the great career that Sara had renounced several years earlier. As for Elizabeth's father, he was conspicuous by his absence. Cold and distant, he found it difficult to assert himself in a milieu dominated by his wife. It is known that the relationship between Elizabeth's parents was far from sunny and a friend of the family adds that the couple had serious 'sexual problems': 'When I dined with Francis one evening, he told me that he had homosexual tendencies and that he had had adventures with young men.' Later Elizabeth was to say about her father, 'My dad and I didn't really become close until after I'd left home.' [Spoto] A euphemistic statement, given that even after her departure, their relationship was always, at best, courteous and polite. In reality, her father never managed to share anything with his daughter while she, influenced by her mother, never understood him.

From the age of four Elizabeth learned to ride and was seized with a passion for animals. Victor Cazalet, a wealthy family friend, presented her with a pony and the little girl immediately proved to be a gifted rider, a talent that would be useful in her early days in Hollywood. Leaving nothing to chance, Sara also signed up her daughter for dancing lessons. Under such maternal pressure, Elizabeth became very retiring and relatives would say that she was 'paralysed by timidity'. However, at the age of four, having taken a bow after a stage performance with other dancers she decided to remain alone on stage bowing to the audience. According to her mother, the public gave her an ovation and several curtain calls, an intoxicating experience for mother and daughter alike.

This gilded life in England ended in early 1939 when war seemed imminent, and the family decided that it would be safer to return to America. Sara, Howard and Elizabeth left for the States while Francis stayed behind for a few months to wind-up his business affairs and close his uncle's gallery. Mother and children sailed to America, arriving in Manhattan then travelling by train to Pasadena, California, where Sara's father lived. No doubt Sara, who had always dreamed of making a success in movies, had a plan: 1939 was the era of child stars such as Shirley Temple and Judy Garland. Perhaps Elizabeth, still only seven, would follow in their footsteps?

When Francis rejoined them at the end of 1939, he opened a new gallery in Hollywood and the Taylor family settled into a large ocean-side house at Pacific Palisades, a fashionable location that was home to many major figures in the movie industry, enabling Elizabeth's mother to make some useful connections. However the young Elizabeth was not particularly gifted and, at eight years old, had neither the physique nor the personality to stand out from the child actors who thronged the studios. When Elizabeth arrived in California her classmates mocked her pronounced English accent, shaming her into quickly changing it – to the extent that she would go on to pronounce her 'a's 'almost as if she were Texan', according to a reporter who met her at the time. Tractable and malleable, the little girl was able to transform herself at will, never really knowing who she really was. She was capable of 'acting', 'becoming', but never developed a true 'ego' or sense of self, something that would have a fundamentally destructive impact on her throughout her life.

In 1940 the family moved to 703 North Elm Drive, Beverly Hills, to be closer to Francis's gallery and the studios. With her daughter's future career as an actress in mind, Sara enrolled the eight-year-old in singing, dancing and riding classes. The child had no friends and would ultimately be deprived of a proper childhood. 'When was I really a child?' she later asked, sadly. But Sara ruled the situation and was all-in-all to her daughter, who would later say of her, 'my mother was my best friend, my counsellor, my inspiration, my faithful confidant.'

Sara dragged her daughter to every neighbourhood entertainment, hoping that she would be seen by everyone in this smart world. She would order her to sing but, to the dismay of her mother and her guests, the child performed timidly, with a quavering voice. Elizabeth later said, 'I never wanted to be an actress; it was forced on me.' Nervous and unsure of herself, the little girl was hardly convincing as the new Shirley Temple, but Sara, undiscouraged, arranged a meeting with a senior Metro-Goldwyn-Mayer producer who invited the family on a tour of the studios. During the visit, the little girl met Louis B. Mayer, the head of MGM, who asked her to sing. Elizabeth performed and Mayer, the busy executive, said: 'Sign her up!'

The contract never arrived. Had Mayer simply changed his mind? Or had he issued his order simply to get rid of a pushy mother? Whatever the reason, Sara refused to be discouraged and on 21 April 1941 she managed to get a contract from Universal Studios for her daughter. The six-month contract guaranteed a weekly salary of $100 for 20 weeks, to be paid to the young actress's mother. Ninety per cent of the money would be placed in an account in the child's name, with her mother pocketing a not-negligible salary of ten per cent.

At this time, Universal's reputation was much lower than that of MGM and Elizabeth burst into tears on her first day of filming, wailing 'But I wanted to be with MGM!' Her wish would soon be granted and in the meantime, while waiting to be cast, the child went daily to the studios where she attended classes like all the other young actors. The young Elizabeth got most of her schooling in this classroom, which provided only a rudimentary education. 'Poor Elizabeth,' Richard Burton used to say later, gently mocking her, 'She was educated at MGM.' This flimsy education left her with an inferiority complex that remained for much of her life. A pupil who studied with her during this time said that Elizabeth was 'painfully shy', that she distrusted the studio heads and that she did not 'like people'.

In summer 1941, the nine-year-old Elizabeth made her first film, an uninteresting comedy called *There's One Born Every Minute*. In one of history's ironies, the casting director commented on Elizabeth, 'The kid has nothing. Her eyes are too old. She doesn't have the face of a kid.' [Spoto] Perhaps it was simply that she was not suited to this trifling role of a badly behaved child. Be that as it may, in September 1941 her future as an actress did not look promising; she was dismissed and her contract was not renewed. Although this disappointing experience did nothing to boost her self-confidence Elizabeth was happy to resume a normal existence and to go back to her school and her classmates. When asked what she would like to be, she replied, 'a ballerina … a nurse … a veterinarian … the first female fire-engine driver. My father is very much against my being an actress.' [Spoto]

But the father's wishes counted for nothing in the Taylor household. Through a friend of her husband Sara learned that MGM was searching for a young girl with an English accent to play a small part in *Lassie Come Home*, the first film of a series starring a dog. Thanks to her perfect British accent and her extraordinary eyes Elizabeth finally got the part, although her mother was chagrined to discover that her name did not feature in the film posters and that she appeared in only four short sequences, for less than ten minutes. No matter, she now had a one-year contract with the prestigious MGM. Studio heads wanted to dye her hair and pluck her eyebrows but the child showed great character and perspicacity. 'They even wanted to remove my mole!' she exclaimed later. 'That became my trademark! They wanted to change the shape of my mouth, my eyebrows – and I said no.' [Spoto]

When she finished filming *Lassie Come Home*, MGM had no other part for her so in summer 1943 she was 'loaned out', as was the custom of the time, to 20th Century Fox, for a film of *Jane Eyre*. Once again, her appearance passed unnoticed and her name did not appear in the credits.

At this time (and in fact throughout most of her life) Elizabeth felt very much alone. Lacking companions, she transferred all her affection to the animals with which she surrounded herself from now on – dogs, cats, chipmunks, horses – conveying the impression of a wild, mysterious child that her press agents were quick to exploit.

In autumn 1943, she was cast in MGM's *White Cliffs of Dover,* a B-movie about the British war effort. Once again, her presence barely registered on screen. Then the studio announced that the head of its talent department, Lucille Carroll, was looking for a young actress who could ride to star in *National Velvet*, an adaptation of Enid Bagnold's best-selling novel. The part was unsuitable for Katharine Hepburn, Vivien Leigh or even Shirley Temple and MGM decided to launch a nationwide search.

Here Elizabeth's future began. Even though she was only 11, the little girl already had quite a temperament. She marched into Lucille Carroll's office and cheekily announced 'I don't know why you're wasting your time. I'm going to play Velvet!' [Spoto] After all she loved horses, was an excellent rider and could carry off the character's British accent to perfection. Why not give her the chance? But Lucille Carroll thought her too young, too small and 'not really ready' for this part. 'How?' asked the offended youngster. It was explained to her with true Hollywood frankness that young Velvet should have a bust and 'you're as flat as a boy.' In response, Elizabeth embarked on a diet (high in protein and carbohydrate) and exercise regime. It was so successful that several months later, when Lucille Carroll returned empty handed from her nationwide search, she found in her office an Elizabeth who had grown 10 cm (4 inches) and who proclaimed unabashed, 'Look! I have boobs!' And so Elizabeth Taylor landed her first major role in the movies. Although she had just turned 12, she had learned how to make-up and to control her voice (especially to speak lower); chameleon-like, Elizabeth was miraculously transformed into an adolescent.

Filming began in February 1944 and the new 'child-woman' (a role she would embody during the first part of her career) immediately displayed charisma and great professionalism. Although she had never taken any real acting lessons, Elizabeth seemed to have acting in her blood: as soon as the cameras started rolling, the young girl assumed her part and gave solid proof of an incredible talent. As Clarence Brown, director of *National Velvet*, explained, 'something magical happened between Elizabeth and the camera. George Cukor once said one day that it's the camera that chooses the star. You can't tell in advance who the camera will love. In *National Velvet,* the camera loved Elizabeth Taylor and that love never failed thereafter.' When filmgoers saw her on the screen alongside Mickey Rooney they fell immediately under the spell of this vital young girl with her expressive face and well-defined figure; from then on she was 'America's little sweetheart'. The critics raved: 'Elizabeth Taylor appeared as one of the year's most extraordinary revelations.'

When *National Velvet* was released, Elizabeth's life was turned upside down and the following day she was a celebrity, with photographers, autograph-hunters and thousands of love-letters descending on her. Elizabeth enjoyed her first experience of fame and was soon invited, along with other Hollywood actors, to the White House where she met President Harry Truman.

Soon her face began to appear in advertisements for Lux soap and Max Factor beauty products, on greeting-cards and even in a series of colouring-books. How would this 12-year-old girl cope with this sudden adulation and what effect would this precocious success have on her personality? One thing is certain, she quickly perfected her seductive powers, knowing that from now on this would be her main weapon.

Elizabeth now became the chief breadwinner of the Taylor family. Just before she turned 13 in February 1945 the publicity department of MGM announced a memorable surprise for her birthday: she was to be presented with the horse she rode in *National Velvet*, to which she had become passionately attached. From that day nothing in the Elizabeth's life would be left to chance, everything would be designed to publicize her. The studios, who knew the commercial worth of their actress, gave her a $7500 bonus and renewed her contract for seven years. The little girl's self-confidence increased and when she didn't like something she did not hesitate to bawl out Louis B. Mayer, yelling at him 'You and your studio can both go to hell!' [Spoto] She was quick-witted and plain speaking, in fact the saltiness that was an integral part of her personality was already firmly in place.

Meanwhile Sara was in heaven: dozens of photos of Elizabeth, alone or accompanied by her mother, covered the walls of every room in the house, as if father and son did not exist. Francis, on the other hand, disapproved (although always in a rather passive fashion) of his daughter's activities. It seems that there was an increasing lack of communication between husband and wife and that they were beginning to grow apart.

It was a year before MGM had another part to offer their new little recruit. No matter, since Elizabeth still got paid; she continued her three hours of schooling every day and wrote melancholy verses addressed to her pony. The press agents seized on this image of an angelic and solitary little girl surrounded by her pets and told her to keep a diary of her adventures with her chipmunk. *Nibbles and Me*, published in 1946, guaranteed publicity for her new film. Nothing was left to chance.

The young starlet lived under constant supervision since the studios expected their little celebrities to behave like model children. According to Elizabeth, this existence was not quite as idyllic as it seemed: 'My life was not my own. The studio and my parents formed a conspiracy to protect my innocence. I couldn't go to the ladies' room on the lot without my mother or the teacher accompanying me. They were convinced I would be attacked. They meant well but it was such an invasion of my sense of self that I felt as if I were living under a microscope.' [Spoto]

In spring 1946 Elizabeth was loaned to Warner Bros. to film *Life with Father*, a comedy in which she had only a small part. In autumn the situation between her parents worsened, to the extent that Sara and Francis decided to separate. The true reason for the split soon emerged – during filming of *Life with Father*, Sara had fallen in love with the film's director, Michael Curtiz. Still close, mother and daughter moved to a beach house at Malibu. Throughout her life, Elizabeth, who didn't seem much affected by the break, would retain the image of a remote paternal figure and always had the disagreeable feeling that her father had never really loved her – a lack of love that she sought to overcome and to compensate for at any price. She would say of this separation, 'The loss wasn't great. These were the years when I felt like an orphan. *My real* fathers were Jules Goldstone, my agent, and Benny Thau, head of talent at MGM. These were the people I looked to for help and advice.'

It was also during this period that the young actress realized the role of cinema in her existence. After a row with her mother she wrote her a significant note:

'I have thought a lot and I see that making films is my whole life. If I gave it up I would be like a tree with its roots cut – I would wither and die.'

The sweet little girl was also rapidly becoming a beautiful young woman; her figure was developing and her beauty became simply breathtaking, although boys of her own age were intimidated by her sex-appeal.

At last she was given star billing in *Cynthia*, a film in which she also had her first screen kiss. As so often, fiction and reality were superimposed; the title role of a sickly girl overprotected by her anxious parents strangely resembled Elizabeth's own life. It's disturbing to think that the adolescent actress developed her identity by imagining that life would play out like a Hollywood screenplay, running on well-oiled wheels. The illusion and magic of the cinema would become her reality, a grounding that would soon have devastating repercussions. She also saw clearly that she would gain her independence only by growing up even faster, 'to find a place away from both my parents' house and the studio'. [Spoto]

In summer 1947 the 15-year-old Elizabeth was interviewed on radio by Louella Parsons, one of Hollywood's leading gossip columnists, to whom she confided that she wanted to become a great actress, 'but most of all I really want to snare a husband'. [Spoto] That is just what she did – and would again throughout her life. 'I was brought up by a very puritanical, moral family,' she explained, 'and I just couldn't adjust to having affairs.' As she said later about this period, 'I had the body of a woman and the emotions of a child.' [Spoto]

Wanting to retain absolute control over the lives of their celebrities, the studio decided to send Sara and her daughter away from Hollywood to escape the rumours that began to collect around the Taylor family. At that time, separations and divorces made bad publicity for the dream factory. Mother and daughter spent the summer in London before returning to Los Angeles when MGM cast Elizabeth in a small part in *A Date with Judy* and then in *Julia Misbehaves*, two forgettable films. For her 16th birthday her parents gave her a present worthy of an American princess, a new Cadillac convertible with a golden key. Nevertheless, during the winter of 1947–1948 the most beautiful and spoilt child-woman in America suffered a worrying depression. Neither diamonds nor the most extravagant presents could satisfy her for long.

Princess Elizabeth in the kingdom of Nicky Hilton

In 1948 the 16-year-old Elizabeth was an attractive young woman with one fixed idea: as in all the films that formed the basis of her life experience, she was searching for a Prince Charming. One day Doris Kearns, her press agent, lunched with Elizabeth and her mother in their Malibu beach house. She brought along Glenn Davis, a charming 23-year-old sportsman. He made an immediate impression, as Elizabeth said later: 'I took one look at him and thought, "O ye gods, no!" He was so wonderful.' [Spoto] In Los Angeles to make a film about his football career, Glenn had just completed military training, and was to be sent to Korea in September. The studio's publicists spotted a love story that would focus a lot of attention on their young star. Glenn represented the perfect America hero that all Midwest girls dreamed of and their two-year separation would give Elizabeth time to grow up while retaining her virginal image. The platonic romance lasted throughout the summer and the handsome footballer marked their friendship by buying Elizabeth a necklace of 69 cultured pearls, saying 'A present fit for a star'. It was her first gift of jewellery but would not be the last. Thanks to Doris Kearns this simple little romance was blown up into a great love story by the media. Before leaving for Korea, Glenn gave his sweetheart his football shirt, in which Elizabeth posed for the press. But Sara did not find the handsome sportsman quite to her taste; after all her daughter earned far more money and a great career seemed open to her.

Elizabeth now played Amy in *Little Women*, a mawkish film in which she made little impression. MGM then sent her to London for her first adult leading role in *The Conspirator,* an uninspired thriller saved only by the quality and freshness of the young actress's interpretation. Although Elizabeth had not had any real acting training, her extensive theatrical and cinema experience since childhood enabled her to know instinctively how to position herself before the cameras, how she should be lighted or how to show off her voluptuous shape and disturbing glance. 'I never had an acting lesson and I didn't know how to act *per se*. I just developed as an actress. Acting is instinctive with me. It's mostly concentration ... Usually it isn't at all hard to get a character. Mostly, I just read my lines through three times at night and then I go to sleep like a log and don't think about anything. I don't sit down and figure should I do this gesture or should I do that. I know it sounds funny for me to say, but it just seems easy, that's all.' [Spoto]

In London Elizabeth and her mother met the Queen and (more excitingly for Elizabeth) British matinee idol Michael Wilding. Twenty years her senior, Wilding was an attractive, highly cultured man who had worked for Hitchcock and was a major stage star. While the young actress may not have made a big impression at the time, he would get to know her better a few years later.

Filming over, Elizabeth and her mother went shopping in Paris before returning to the US in February 1949. In New York they met up with her father, now more or less reconciled with his wife, and the 'united' family then went to stay with Francis's uncle, Howard Young, in Florida, where the young star celebrated her 17th birthday. It was here that she met her first fiancé, William D. Pawley Jr., ten years older (an important detail) and scion of a wealthy family. Elizabeth declared herself to be 'infatuated with being in love'. Meanwhile, in the style of a low-budget soap opera, Glenn Davis, her handsome footballer serving in Korea, was on leave in California and wanted to fly to meet her in Florida. The actress could hardly refuse and journalists and photographers turned up at the airport to record this scoop, tipped off by MGM's press department. But Elizabeth had little time for Glenn and Pawley took advantage of the break-up to propose, although making it clear that he expected her to give up her career as an actress and that he would not tolerate reporters or his 'future wife's' provocative décolletages. At first Elizabeth acquiesced: her fiancé was 'hot-blooded', 'decisive', had 'character' and had also proved that he was capable of 'taking charge of her'. Paley seemed the reverse of her cold, self-effacing, passive father.

None of this prevented her from getting together the following month with the handsome Glenn Davis in Hollywood, where the 'model couple' were due to attend the Academy Awards. Elizabeth mounted the stage in a magnificent, low-cut gown to present the Oscar for Best Costume. At 17, more beautiful than ever, she was voted Miss Junior America and named Princess of the Jewellery Council's 1949 Diamond Jubilee. When she naively asked the organizers if she could keep the $22,000 diamond tiara, they had to explain that, alas, this was not possible.

In June William Pawley presented her with an engagement ring featuring an enormous diamond and Sara announced to the press that the wedding would take place in spring 1950. Elizabeth added that she and her husband would live in Florida: 'In Hollywood, I could never be anything but Elizabeth Taylor, but in Miami, I'll be Elizabeth Pawley – and I'll like that [Spoto].' However, from spring 1949 the despotic attitude of her future husband had begun to weigh heavily on her. In August MGM cast her in *The Big Hangover* as a wealthy boss's daughter who falls in love with an alcoholic soldier. When Pawley visited her in California, he was not pleased to learn that Elizabeth had signed for another film and announced that he wanted her to quit this 'unhealthy' profession immediately. Their disagreement had severe consequences: Pawley returned to Florida and the following morning it was announced that the engagement was at an end.

Elizabeth spent the evening at the Mocambo, one of Hollywood's smartest nightclubs, listening to singer Vic Damone. Press rumours of 'a new love story' flew, but the evening was more notable for the presence of a certain Nicky Hilton, who immediately fell for the radiant Elizabeth's charm, and who would quickly take an important place in her life.

No man could remain indifferent to the young actress, whose figure turned all heads. Minute details of her vital statistics were publicised by the press: height, 1.64 m (5ft 4½ inches); waist, 57 cm (22 inches) ; bust and hips, 90 cm (35 inches), while Technicolor made the most of her violet eyes with their brown iris, shaded by long dark lashes, the delicacy of her skin, her porcelain complexion and the alluring little mole on her right cheek. All of America was in love with her.

Around this time MGM loaned their starlet to Paramount to play opposite Montgomery Clift in *A Place in the Sun*, adapted from Theodore Dreiser's novel and directed by the legendary George Stevens.

At first sight, Taylor and Clift had only their beauty in common. Monty was walking wounded, with serious psychological problems, while Elizabeth was a frivolous young girl, whose only thought was for enjoyment. Nevertheless a great friendship immediately sprang up between the two, a friendship that, for Elizabeth, became disturbing as she fell in love with this man who was 12 years her senior. She was intrigued by the cultivated actor, who hung portraits of Rimbaud, Melville, Dostoyevsky, Baudelaire and Edgar Allan Poe in his rooms. She was probably also troubled by the self-destructive streak in this heavy-drinking, drug-dependent man but it took some time before she could accept that he was attracted only to men. The Method-trained Clift, with his extensive stage experience, became a mentor for the young actress and the film was soon seen as a prototype for the new generation of tortured, passionate actors. Elizabeth's acting was praised and critics did not fail to note the explosive on-screen chemistry between the two stars.

During filming of *A Place in the Sun*, Nicky Hilton courted Elizabeth and she quickly fell in love. He came from a very wealthy family: his twice-married father, owner of the famous hotel chain of the same name, was known for collecting beautiful Hollywood actresses. Very rich, handsome and sure of himself, Nicky was a noted playboy, drinker and gambler. Although Elizabeth's on-screen image was that of a passionate, seductive young woman, she was always chaperoned by her mother and despite her strong will, apparent assurance and the profane language to which she was addicted, she was still genuinely innocent. 'I was married a virgin' [Spoto], she later said.

Invited to stay at the Hilton's Bel-Air mansion and the lavish Hilton hotel, the Taylor family was impressed by the wealth and elegance of their daughter's suitor – the Hilton family owned a chain of 16 hotels worth $80 million. Francis agreed to the young couple's engagement, on condition that they waited until Elizabeth turned 18 and that Elizabeth got her high school diploma before getting married. However the Hilton family and MGM were influential and it did not prove difficult to improvise a graduation ceremony so that she could claim this phoney diploma.

On 21 February 1950 Sara and Francis Taylor held a reception to announce their daughter's engagement. The wedding would take place on 6 May at the Good Shepherd Catholic Church, Beverly Hills.

Elizabeth Taylor's life has frequently mirrored the parts she played on screen. She was now cast as a young girl about to be married to a society boy in *Father of the Bride*, an accomplished comedy directed by Vicente Minnelli. MGM, never reluctant to exploit their star's private life to promote her films, was delighted by this unexpected marriage that seemed so timely. The studio paid all wedding expenses and Elizabeth's wedding dress was designed by MGM's costume designer. Once again, reality merged with cinema fiction and everything was orchestrated, down to the release of the film shortly after her wedding.

On the great day, 2500 people gathered outside the Beverly Hills church to watch the bride and groom, choking the pavements of Santa Monica Boulevard. The police could do little to control the crowd but the situation was saved from chaos when the newlyweds entered the limousine that awaited them outside the church. Seven hundred guests, naturally including Hollywood's A-list, were invited to the reception at the Bel-Air Hotel. The following day the young couple slipped away to Pebble Beach, before leaving for Europe. There are no happy anecdotes about their honeymoon: Nicky spent his time drinking, gambling and exploding in rage until finally the lovers ended up in separate rooms. The handsome playboy drank so heavily that the marriage was not consummated until the third night. When she returned to the US, Elizabeth had lost ten kilos (22 lbs), seemed utterly downcast and soon began suffering migraines and colitis. Her fairytale had rapidly turned into a sordid nightmare. Much later she revealed that Nicky Hilton was a wife-beater. 'He became sullen, angry and abusive,' she said, without giving details. Traces of blows and her bruised arms told the tale, however, but Elizabeth was so ashamed of the failure of her marriage that she complained neither to her friends nor her mother, from whom she gently but firmly distanced herself.

On her return from this brief honeymoon, MGM quickly put their star to work in *Father's Little Dividend*, a sequel to *Father of the Bride*, where she played the part of a young mother. For the first time her screen life seemed to depart from reality, since Elizabeth had a miscarriage and there would be no child from this marriage.

MGM had masterminded the romance and then the wedding; it now orchestrated the inevitable separation. Soon the public read the star's press announcement that 'Nicky and I have come to a final parting of the ways. There

is no possibility of a reconciliation.' After a Palm Springs holiday with her mother, Elizabeth returned to her parents' home in Beverly Hills.

At the same time she started work on *Love is Better than Ever*, an ironically titled movie, since love was not on the star's agenda. When filming ended in December 1950 she filed for divorce on the grounds of 'extreme mental cruelty'. In court she declared that her husband had become 'violent' and that he had used 'abusive language' but did not mention the physical abuse she had endured. She waived alimony but asked for the return of her maiden name. Her requests were accepted and the divorce was soon granted. Elizabeth, not yet 20, viewed this disastrous experience as her first great failure.

However she quickly rebounded from this divorce, according to Louella Parsons, the famous gossip columnist, who announced that Stanley Donen, director of *Love is Better than Ever*, had not lost time in paying assiduous court to Elizabeth. When he heard about it, Nicky Hilton was wild with rage and spitefully told the press 'Every man deserves the opportunity of sleeping with Elizabeth Taylor and at the rate she's going every man will.'

While Elizabeth could not bear to be alone, neither could she bear to live with her parents any longer. At first she decided to move into her lawyer's guest-room before moving to a comfortable little apartment in Westwood, not far from UCLA, with her secretary Peggy Rutledge as her companion. By spring 1951 Elizabeth's nervous condition led to gastric problems and doctors prescribed a diet of baby-food. Agitated, depressed, anxious and exhausted she smoked more than ever. She lost a lot of weight and became uncharacteristically flat-chested.

In the meantime, press speculation continued about an engagement between Elizabeth and Stanley Donen, who was living apart from his wife. MGM viewed these rumours with apprehension; it was, after all, only the early 1950s, a period when strict moral codes could break the career of any actor thought to be promiscuous. Although uneasy, the studio offered their star a new seven-year contract to run until 1958, with a not-inconsiderable salary of $5000 per week; her mother would continue to draw 10 per cent of this handsome sum. To put paid to the rumours, MGM decided to despatch Elizabeth to England and away from Stanley Donen. Accompanied by Peggy Rutledge – and not, for the first time, by her overbearing mother – Elizabeth departed for London, where she was to film *Ivanhoe*, a big-budget movie inspired by Sir Walter's sweeping romantic novel. The film was commercially successful but Elizabeth seemed completely lifeless throughout and her acting was worse than mediocre.

A Prince Charming with British reserve

In spring 1951 Elizabeth renewed her acquaintance with Michael Wilding, the handsome and distinguished English actor she had admired so much when they had met several years earlier. On her return to the US in October she was suddenly feeling much better. It was the age-old remedy: cure the sickness with the sickness; once again she had fallen in love.

Michael, who celebrated his 39th birthday with Elizabeth and a few friends, was at the time one of England's best-known actors, having first made his name on the stage and later in the cinema. Handsome, elegant and refined, he was both a gentleman and a ladies' man. When Elizabeth arrived in London in early summer, Michael was romancing Marlene Dietrich who was madly in love with him. Elizabeth, with the determination for which she is known, decided that *she* wanted this handsome, seductive man but he remained cool and distant. Another troubling detail was that he was still married to Kay Young (like Stanley Donen, he lived apart from his wife). Elizabeth, however, was not in the least discouraged. In reality she and Michael could not have been more different and it is undoubtedly true that what attracted her, as she said later, was that 'he represented tranquillity, security, maturity – all the things I needed in myself.' [Spoto] The complete opposite to Nicky Hilton.

Prudently, Michael kept his distance, arguing that he was too old for her and that it was best not to rush into things. Obstinately, she persisted. In autumn, when the filming of *Ivanhoe* finished, Elizabeth returned to the US and installed herself in a suite at the Plaza Hotel, New York. Realizing that she could use the press to achieve her aim, she had herself photographed in a nightclub with her great friend Montgomery Clift and, more disquietingly, walking in New England with her ex-husband. Michael Wilding saw the photos in the English tabloids and immediately fell into the trap: mad with jealousy he telephoned Elizabeth, who seemed to have won her campaign. She managed to persuade Michael to join her between two movies in Las Vegas and Louella Parsons headed her 12 December gossip-column 'LIZ, WILDING IN LAS VEGAS'.

Wilding's wife saw that the situation was more serious that it had appeared and now agreed to divorce him. When she heard the news Elizabeth lost no time; that same evening, while they dined in a luxurious Los Angeles restaurant, Michael offered her a diamond ring although he had no intention of proposing to her. Once again, however, he underestimated her quick wit, as he later recounted humorously. 'I reached for her right hand but she snatched it away, putting out her left hand and waggling her third finger. "That's where it belongs," she said. Then, admiring the ring, she kissed me and said, "That makes it official, doesn't it? Or shall I spell it out for you? Dear Mr Shilly-Shally, will you marry me?"' [Spoto] After all, Michael was now officially single and Elizabeth's divorce would soon be made absolute.

Intent on protecting their star's reputation while profiting from the publicity generated by this new scandal, MGM announced that Elizabeth would make her next film with Michael Wilding. When she arrived at the studios for a costume fitting, it was seen that she had regained all the weight she had earlier lost; she was sent to Palm Springs to burn it off with drastic dieting. On 17 February 1952 MGM officially announced the news of her forthcoming marriage and Elizabeth immediately flew to rejoin Michael in London where, on 21 February, the lovers were discreetly married at Caxton Hall, Westminster. 'I am glad to be British again' declared Elizabeth, smiling broadly at the crowd of onlookers who awaited her as she exited the Registry Office. The next day the pair left for their honeymoon in the Swiss Alps.

Bad news awaited the couple on their return to London: Michael learned that he had to pay a tax bill of £40,000, wiping out his finances. Suddenly the great cinema idol was broke and financially dependent on his wife.

In summer 1952 MGM cast Elizabeth in *The Girl Who Had Everything*, a creaky melodrama that again seemed to mirror the star's real life. She played a rich, pet-loving girl who falls in love with a violent husband, just as in her first marriage. During filming, it was discovered that Elizabeth was five months pregnant and cameramen and the costume department had to do their best to hide her expanding waistline. The Wildings were thrilled, although their financial situation was precarious. MGM could not come up with a film that interested Michael Wilding and Elizabeth would not be paid during her pregnancy leave. In a piece of miraculous timing, Elizabeth was finally eligible to access to the $47,000 she had earned during her career as a child actress, which had been held in trust for her until she came of age. MGM agreed to lend them the additional $28,000 they needed to buy the house of their dreams, high up in Beverly Hills. Nevertheless Elizabeth felt humiliated at having to beg for money: 'The bastards! They made me feel it was a crime to have a child instead of making movies. I had to go on bended knees. I'll never again ask anyone for money.' The couple's finances were tight from the end of summer 1952 until spring 1953 and they lived quietly in their snug two-bedroom nest, surrounded by a large garden and, naturally, all sorts of pets.

It was during this relatively lean period of plenitude and calm that Michael Howard Wilding was born in early 1953. When Elizabeth was told that a caesarean was necessary, she reacted with surprising composure. A part-time nanny was hired and debts continued to accumulate. It was time to go back to work.

Despite their tight finances, the Wildings entertained guests such as Spencer Tracy, Gene Kelly, Judy Garland and Errol Flynn at their villa, invariably sending-out for food – Elizabeth, being a modern woman and a Hollywood diva, did not see herself as cook or housekeeper. At one Sunday afternoon pool party, the Wildings met a certain Richard Burton, a 26-year-old Welsh actor who had just arrived in Hollywood. Tall and sturdy, with a beautiful deep voice, he seemed very self-assured and it was rumoured that he was very talented. Burton would later write of this first meeting, 'She was, I decided, the most astonishingly self-contained, pulchritudinous, remote, inaccessible woman I had ever seen. She spoke to no one. She looked at no one. She steadily kept on reading her book. Was she merely sullen? I thought not. There was no trace of sulkiness in the divine face. [...] Her breasts were apocalyptic, they would topple empires down before they withered. Indeed, her body was a miracle of construction and the work of an engineer of genius.' [Spoto]

Although married, the Welsh actor was immediately attracted to this disquieting American beauty and took advantage of an opportune moment to approach her. He was astonished to hear this goddess of unearthly beauty unleash a string of obscenities and, when questioned, told her 'You have a remarkable command of Old English [Spoto].' Testing the waters, he then explained that he came from a culture where 'such words are an indication of weakness in vocabulary and emptiness of mind' [Spoto]. But Elizabeth was unimpressed and put him in his place by turning away. She would not see him again for several years.

Despite this ostensibly peaceful life, Elizabeth and Michael began to draw away from each other. Elizabeth had been wrong in assuring her husband that his career would not suffer in Hollywood. She nagged him for not spending time with his son and for failing to show her affection; she was less and less able to tolerate what she now saw as his passivity and coldness. One morning when Michael was quietly filling in a crossword, Elizabeth snatched the newspaper from him, ripped it up and threw it in the fire. She tried to jolt him from his British reserve by taunting him to hit her, to which Michael responded that he had 'never gone in for hitting hysterical females'. Exasperated, Elizabeth retorted 'Oh, God, if only you would! At least that would prove you are flesh and blood instead of a stuffed dummy!' [Spoto]

While distancing herself from her husband, Elizabeth spent more and more time with her close friend Montgomery Clift. Naturally the scandal sheets jumped to rumours of an affair – an unlikely assumption, obviously.

Just when the Wilding's financial situation was becoming critical, Elizabeth heard that Vivien Leigh was suffering from deep depression and would be unable to finish filming *Elephant Walk*. She would have to be replaced. MGM loaned Elizabeth's services to Paramount and she immediately began work on this adventure film, made in Technicolor. At the end of production, a fan blew a piece of metal into her eye; an urgent operation was necessary and she was advised to spend the weekend quietly to allow the scar to heal. But Elizabeth could not resist playing with her son, who accidentally landed a blow on her eye and she was obliged to return to hospital. The situation was critical and the doctors feared that she would lose the sight in this now severely damaged eye. As with her caesarean, Elizabeth remained calm and once again reassured Michael, with the 'blind' optimism that undoubtedly gave her strength in facing the most difficult situations.

Two weeks later, completely recovered, she went back to work in *Rhapsody*, a melodrama that, according to Elizabeth, should 'never have gone before the camera'. Next she took a brief holiday in Denmark before starting work on *Beau Brummell* in London. Exhausted, she came down with 'flu. The press had a field-day: she was having a nervous breakdown; she was paralyzed; she was dying of a heart attack or of pneumonia. Elizabeth did nothing to refute the rumours since, as they say in Hollywood, there's no such thing as bad publicity. Once recovered, she started shooting *Beau Brummell*, another failure. Her situation was made worse by the fact that on her arrival in London Elizabeth found that all her jewels (including pearls, rubies and emeralds) had been stolen during the flight.

On their return to Los Angeles the Wildings were invited to present the Oscar for Best Documentary at the Academy Awards. Her hair short and wearing an elegant dress, Elizabeth looked more beautiful than ever. By early summer she was again pregnant and the couple moved to a larger house with a pool higher up in Beverly Hills, with a splendid view. The enormous house was designed in contemporary style: one of the living-room walls was made of bark from which grew ferns. Elizabeth, who loved informality, walked around barefoot, dropping clothes and possessions anywhere, exasperating her more meticulous husband. 'Her untidiness has always been her chief fault,' he commented later, with some acerbity. Now the Wildings had a cook, nanny, gardeners and a secretary, but Michael consistently refused the films he was offered and it fell to Elizabeth to earn enough to support their lavish lifestyle.

It was at this point that she was offered what promised to be a fantastic role, certainly the best since *A Place in the Sun*. Based on F. Scott Fitzgerald's story 'Babylon Revisited', *The Last Time I Saw Paris* was directed by the legendary Richard Brooks. Unfortunately the final result was disappointing and the beautiful, violet-eyed star had to wait for her next film, *Giant,* before she could prove her great acting talent.

On 27 February 1955, her own birthday, Elizabeth's second son, Christopher Edward Wilding, was born. She had to have another caesarean, although this delivery was easier than the previous one. Her salary was again suspended while she recovered, so she was pleased to learn that her old friend George Stevens, director of *A Place in the Sun*, wanted her for the female lead in *Giant*, a Warner Bros. production. This saga was to run for more than three hours, covering a 30-year period, and Elizabeth played a young and innocent woman at the beginning of the film, ageing into a grey-haired (beautiful) grandmother at the end. She was 23, *Giant* was her first major film and it became one of her greatest successes, winning critical acclaim for her remarkable acting. This, her 25th feature film, was also one of the longest and most exacting projects of her career. It was partly shot in Burbank, but also on location in Virginia and Texas, in high summer, with temperatures often hitting 49 °C (120 °F). The open, easygoing Elizabeth quickly made friends with Rock Hudson and James Dean, both gay, although the two men did not hit it off and she had to spend her time alternately with one or the other, often drinking until the early hours and listening to their problems and worries. She was the only member of the cast to bond with the 24-year-old James Dean, whose temperament was dark and explosive. She flirted with Rock Hudson and soon fell in love with him until she realised that he would never succumb to her charms. At a time when homosexuality was inadmissible and might wreck a career, Elizabeth was one of the first to show that she had no problem with it. 'The creativity of homosexuals has made so much possible in this town, in all the arts. Take out the homosexuals and there's no Hollywood!' she later stated, at the risk of shocking puritanical America.

Elizabeth's health was not at its best during filming; she first suffered from sciatica, then angina and stomach pains. James Dean finished his part and left the picture; on his departure, 26 September, Elizabeth presented him with a Siamese cat as a token of friendship. Four days later, while viewing the day's rushes, she learned the terrible news. To celebrate a new nine-film contract, Dean had bought himself a magnificent metallic-grey Porsche. Driving at almost a hundred miles an hour, he had a head-on collision with a Ford at the intersection of Highways 41 and 466 near Paso Robles, north of Los Angeles. He died on the spot. Elizabeth, devastated by the news, had to stop filming and was admitted to hospital. It was a fortnight before she was able to return to the set to complete her final shots.

The Wilding's marital situation did not improve. From autumn 1955 the couple slept in separate rooms. The fact is that since their first meeting Elizabeth had changed a lot. She had become assertive, both in her private life and in her career. Michael, for his part, was now only a shadow of what he had been and nobody was interested in him. He had become someone condescendingly called Mr Elizabeth Taylor.

James Dean's death marked Elizabeth deeply and she succumbed to a fierce depression when the filming of *Giant* ended. When she celebrated her 24th birthday in February 1956, she gave the impression of being bored with everything. She longed for passion, excitement, folly, and it was obvious that Michael was not the man to satisfy her. Husband and wife led separate social lives and became virtually strangers to each other. Elizabeth spent more and more time with Montgomery Clift. Although he was an alcoholic and dependent on every kind of drug, she felt that he was the only person who could understand her. She had seen the dangerous effect of drugs on Monty and steered clear of them but she discovered that her tolerance for alcohol was good and that she could often drink her guests under the table. In her depression she ate huge quantities of food and put on weight alarmingly. She would struggle with her weight all her life. 'My taste buds get in an uproar,' she said, 'and I get a lusty, sensual thing out of eating.' [Spoto] She was hungry and thirsty for entertainment, men, alcohol, medicine and nourishment of every kind, as if her ferocious appetite could never be assuaged. Montgomery Clift, who tried to warn Elizabeth about her sudden weight-gain, said 'She really became terribly overweight and when she came out in an evening dress, I said "Honey, you're the broadest broad I ever saw!"' [Spoto] With typical good-nature and spontaneity, Elizabeth's reacted by exploding into laughter.

When Michael told his wife that he had turned down a lucrative part in the American tour of *My Fair Lady*, Elizabeth exploded with rage: 'You're nothing but a coward. To think that the man I once loved turns out to be nothing but a coward!' [Spoto] Wilding immediately packed a suitcase and the scene definitively ended their four-year marriage.

Elizabeth was shortly to star in *Raintree County* with Montgomery Clift and needed to begin a crash diet. At some risk to her health, she managed to lose nearly 10 kilos (22 lbs) in less than a fortnight.

On 12 May, after a long day in the studio, Elizabeth invited a few friends to dine with her in the Beverly Hills heights. The party included Rock Hudson, Kevin McCarthy and Montgomery Clift, but Monty was tired and decided to go home early, driving down the long winding road. Driving ahead of him, Kevin McCarthy heard a terrific crash and immediately turned back to find Clift's car had smashed into a telegraph pole. Before lapsing into a coma, Monty murmured to him that he had fallen asleep at the wheel. Elizabeth rushed to the scene and cradled Clift's bloodied head in her lap. Fortunately the accident was not too serious; although the actor sustained a broken nose and jaw they healed in just over two months, during which filming came to a halt. But physical pain served only to increase the actor's dependence on drugs, notably painkillers.

As with *National Velvet*, *A Place in the Sun*, *The Last Time I saw Paris* and *Giant*, Elizabeth enjoyed working on *Raintree County*, and this shows on screen; her interpretation and acting were excellent. Particularly noticeable was the amount of work she had put into her diction: her Southern accent was convincing and would soon come in useful again when she embarked on the female lead in a film inspired by the Southern playwright Tennessee Williams.

Passions and vulgarities of the Queen of Hollywood

Elizabeth was still married to Michael in spring 1956 when she fell in love with Kevin McClory, a young man with a lot of charm. Kevin was assistant director on *Around the World in 80 Days*, produced by Mike Todd. However this passing romance was rapidly eclipsed by the overpowering personality of the fiercely ambitious producer. Mike Todd asked McClory to introduce him to Elizabeth, whereupon he hired a yacht and organized a weekend cruise, inviting the Wildings and several friends.

Mike Todd, who was 49 at the time, was the epitome of the self-made man. He was also an unbridled megalomaniac, who owed his career to good business sense and downright chutzpah. Todd grew up in a Jewish quarter of Minneapolis

and tried his hand at many things – newspaper seller, apprentice pharmacist, building worker and circus crew – before getting married and producing his first music-hall spectacular. He made and lost small fortunes until he managed to produce a series of Broadway spectacles that earned him millions.

In a gambler's throw, he invested all his money in *Around the World in 80 Days*, a super-production to be filmed around the world for more than a year. The film's line-up has never been equalled: it included David Niven, Frank Sinatra, Shirley MacLaine, Marlene Dietrich, Buster Keaton, John Gielgud, Ava Gardner and dozens more. Todd, who had neither the physique of Nicky Hilton nor the refinement of Michael Wilding, looked like a pot-bellied truck driver. He spoke loudly, loading his speech with obscenities, and smoked huge cigars. Above all, he gave the impression that nothing and no one could ever get him down. He was a high liver, a big roller, who spent lavishly and burned the candle at both ends.

Aboard Todd's yacht, Elizabeth drank champagne, sunbathed and paid little attention to her host. Although Todd had lived with the beautiful actress Evelyn Keyes for three years, it seems he had a little plan in mind when he invited the Wildings to dinner, then to a friendly barbecue. He despatched Evelyn to Paris on business and then telephoned to tell her he had fallen in love with Elizabeth Taylor. Resigned, Evelyn wished him good luck before hanging up. On 19 July MGM officially announced in their usual manner that Michael and Elizabeth had separated. The following day Mike Todd asked Elizabeth to meet him at Metro. At first she thought he wanted to offer her a part in a film but quickly realized that he had something much more personal in mind, as she recounted later. 'He spoke very softly for about 45 minutes. He told me that he loved me, that he had been thinking about me constantly and he said he was going to marry me. I sat like a mongoose mesmerized by a cobra. He didn't ask me, he told me. He was irresistible ... I left that office knowing that I would soon be Mrs Michael Todd.' [Spoto] The 27-year age gap made not the slightest difference.

So Elizabeth left a fragile, sensitive, submissive, refined man for this strong, rock-hard, authoritarian, boorish man, with whom she fell violently in love. This epitomizes the actress's love-life – torn between the desire for what she calls a 'real man' and a 'sensitive, gentle, understanding man'. In the arms of Mike Todd, with whom everything moved so fast, she was happy, happier than she had ever been. When she was filming *Raintree County* on location, the ugly Prince Charming flew in his private jet to join his beautiful princess after his day's work, and loaded her with jewels, flowers and furs. He telephoned every evening and presented her with a 20-carat diamond the day he proposed. How could she resist?

Meanwhile, public disapproved of Elizabeth Taylor was growing; she was, after all, married and the mother of two little children. But she refused to allow herself to be touched by negative press, throwing herself body and soul into her new idyll. The two lovers defied morality and intended to live out their romance as it pleased them. During dinner at the home of Eddie Fisher, Todd's best friend, the producer looked lasciviously at Elizabeth and said, in typical style before all the guests 'I'd like to fuck you as soon as I finish this.' [Spoto] Elizabeth simply giggled.

On 27 September 1956, Elizabeth, Rock Hudson and George Stevens were invited to leave their hand- and footprints in the cement outside Grauman's

Chinese Theatre, signalling their supremacy. Elizabeth and Mike then flew to New York for the premiere of *Around the World in 80 Days*, following which, on her lawyer's advice Elizabeth moved to the State of Nevada to accelerate her divorce proceedings. Yet again she told the press that, once married, she would put her career on hold: 'The blending of a career with marriage does not seem to work out satisfactorily. So retirement from maximum activity is the most desirable thing.' [Spoto] And, in fact, after *Raintree County* she did not make another film for more than a year.

Elizabeth appeared before the court on 14 November and charged Michael with 'mental cruelty', following the tradition of the time. Once again she waived alimony. A fortnight later the Wildings' house was sold for $200,000 and Mike Todd and his sweetheart left for a vacation in Florida and the Bahamas. Here Elizabeth slipped and was rushed to hospital back in New York, where it was discovered that she had seriously damaged two spinal disks and that she was pregnant.

Following a spinal graft she was in great pain and had to wear an orthopaedic corset. To comfort her, generous Mike decorated the walls of her hospital room with pictures by Cézanne, Monet, Utrillo and Cassatt, to the value of $315,000. Nothing was too good for his beautiful princess.

While Elizabeth was delighted to be pregnant, the lovers were not yet married and care had to be taken to conceal the compromising bulge. The laws of the period and the slowness of procedures meant that Elizabeth was not yet officially divorced. In January 1957, therefore, she went to Mexico hoping to speed things up. It did, and that is how Mike Todd and Elizabeth Taylor were able to get married on Saturday 2 February in the Mexican villa of Cantinflas, star of *Around the World in 80 Days*. True to form – a small folly among so many others – Mike presented his new wife with a $90,000 diamond bracelet. The Jewish ceremony and the three-day fiesta that followed seemed to come from a Hollywood movie: there was dancing, caviar, lobster, and champagne – vintage, naturally – flowed like water.

The newlyweds then took off for a seaside honeymoon before continuing to party in New York and Palm Springs nightclubs – a party that lasted a whole year since Todd and Taylor never did things by halves. Passionately in love, they fought, shouted and slugged each other before reconciling in bed. Mike himself said that they fought because 'it's so damn much fun to make up again'. 'When she flies into a tantrum, I fly into a bigger one', he declared [Spoto x 2]. And his wife retorted, in typically salty language, 'Tell ole flannelmouth there to stuff it!' [Kelley] Debbie Reynolds, Eddie Fisher's wife, said that Mike beat his wife, 'clobbering her', even 'knocking her to the floor': 'He really hit her! Elizabeth screamed, walloped him right back and from there they went right into a huge fight. Mike dragged her by her hair – while she was screaming and kicking at him – across the room into the foyer. I went running after him, jumping on his back to help Elizabeth. The two of them were slapping each other around [and] I was trying to pull Mike off, shouting at him to stop, and the next thing I knew they were wrestling on the floor, kissing and making up. ... They both got mad at me for interfering ... They were like that during their entire relationship. They loved having a massive fight and then they would make up and make love.' [Spoto] That year, *Around the World in 80 Days* won the Oscar for Best Picture, which for Mike Todd represented an unprecedented achievement and a considerable financial return.

Throughout this period Eddie Fisher and his wife, Debbie Reynolds, were best friends with Elizabeth and Mike. Eddie worshipped Todd, whose manners and style he imitated to a disquieting degree. He admitted that 'I idolized Mike. I wanted to be like him and he became the most important and influential man in my life.' [Spoto] By May Elizabeth had gained a vast amount of weight with her pregnancy, but this did not prevent her accompanying Todd to the Cannes Film Festival, where they rented a villa and invited the Fishers to join them. Eddie Fisher seemed to be increasingly fascinated by the beautiful Elizabeth. From there they all proceeded to London, where Todd threw a huge party for the English premiere of *Around the World in 80 Days*.

On 6 August 1957, Elizabeth gave birth to a little girl, by caesarean as usual. The Todds named her Elizabeth Frances. Little Liza, as she was always known, was premature and did not start breathing until 14 minutes after she was born – 14 minutes that Mike Todd described as being 'the longest of my life'. After two months at home the Todds, always ready for something new, resumed their travels around the world, throwing parties and spending recklessly to promote *Around the World in 80 Days*. In early 1958 Todd had a fit of megalomania (unless it was madness, pure and simple) and decided that Elizabeth deserved an extravagant mission; he decreed that she would become, in the middle of the Cold War, a goodwill ambassadress between America and the USSR. After all, he reasoned, her beauty was the best weapon to counter the Russians' belligerence. Without consulting representatives of the US Government, the Todds prepared to fly to Moscow, with Mike announcing that his wife was 'the best secret weapon we've got' and that once in the USSR 'she would undermine their whole structure', while Elizabeth told journalists she wanted 'to have tea with Khrushchev'. And, amazingly, she did: on 27 January Mike and Elizabeth were invited to a reception where they met Khrushchev in person.

As if that were not enough, Elizabeth decided that diplomatic relations between China and America needed warming up too. Fortunately this improvised and disproportionate role of peace ambassadress quickly collapsed and the Todds moved to the French Riviera (where the food, climate and hotels were a great deal better than in the Communist bloc). Once again Elizabeth told the press that after her next film she would give up her movie career: 'I don't want to be a movie star anymore. I just want to be a wife and mother. I've been an actress for 15 years, now I want to be a woman ... I think the man in the family should drive the car, order the food in restaurants and wear the pants ... '. [Spoto] These seem like old-fashioned and paradoxical statements coming from a woman with a steely temperament and a will of iron. In any case, given the couple's financial situation, it was Elizabeth who 'wore the pants', since her earnings were considerably higher than her husband's – something she did not yet know but would soon find out.

However she still had to postpone playing the little woman at home, as the Todds were badly in need of money after all their lavish expenditure. Elizabeth accepted MGM's next assignment and played the part of Maggie Pollitt in *Cat on a Hot Tin Roof*, adapted from Tennessee Williams' Pulitzer Prize-winning play. 'Maggie was the only aristocrat,' the playwright said about this character She was the only one free of greed. I sympathized with her and liked her, and [she] had become steadily more charming to me as I worked on her characterization.' [Spoto] Directed by Richard Brooks, the film gave Elizabeth one of her greatest roles – as it did to Paul Newman – and earned six Academy Award nominations.

Elizabeth's salary for this film was $125,000, which Mike hoped to invest in his next production.

So do dreams turn into nightmares.

On Friday 21 March 1958 Elizabeth was due to attend a banquet in New York with her husband. They planned to fly in their private plane, the *Lucky Liz*, but Elizabeth had a nasty cold and decided at the last moment to stay at home and rest in view of the long week's filming ahead of her. Mike Todd departed on the *Lucky Liz* with two pilots and a friend. Approaching the Zuni Mountains near Grants in New Mexico, the weather worsened and a dense fog formed. The plane crashed.

There were no survivors. The body of Mike Todd was identified only by his wedding ring, recovered from his charred corpse. Elizabeth and Mike had been married for just over a year.

When she heard the news early the following morning, Elizabeth became hysterical. She screamed, wept and ran from room to room until she was given a large injection of sedatives to calm her down. The funeral took place in a small Illinois town; Elizabeth could hardly stand with grief and was supported by her secretary and doctor.

At the age of 26, Hollywood's most promising actress was a widow. She would later declare that 'I remained totally dependent on Mike's memory for many years after his death.' But she grew close to Eddie Fisher who had venerated Mike Todd, and Eddie did not hesitate to leave his wife for Elizabeth.

Everyone assumed that the late producer was enormously rich, but on his death Elizabeth discovered that she was left with nothing but a tangle of bills and back-taxes. Three children and her parents depended on her, along with numerous staff, secretaries, lawyers, gardeners. She could not stay off work and returned as quickly as possible to the studios to finish filming *Cat on a Hot Tin Roof*. Despite her grief and the surreal nature of her situation, she displayed enormous professionalism, delivering one of the great performances of her career. The film was MGM's biggest hit of 1958. Audience ratings and critics were unanimous: Elizabeth had indeed become Hollywood's greatest star.

The greatest, but also the most controversial: billboards and advertisements for *Cat on a Hot Tin Roof* appeared throughout America, showing Elizabeth wearing only a slip drawn up above her knees and a deep décolletage, provocatively curled up on a bed, reeking of sexuality, while Paul Newman in the background hardly seems to notice her. Elizabeth *was* the cat on a hot tin roof – this time the child-woman was transformed into a femme fatale, a role she would embody from then on, one that fitted her like a glove. Taylor, the femme fatale, was on the one hand the personification of rampant sexuality and on the other hand, the devouring woman, the man-eater, the female cannibal. Sexuality linked with death was a disturbing theme that gripped an America in transition.

Elizabeth lost a lot of weight after her husband's death and lived from one day to the next. While she spent much time with Eddie, every evening she was alone in a vast, silent mansion, and for the first time in her life, as she explained 'I could not sleep. As a result, I began taking sleeping-pills.' She also drank worrying amounts of whisky and took large quantities of medication, an explosive mixture to which she quickly became addicted.

The highs and lows of a merry widow

Eddie Fisher grew up in poverty dreaming of becoming rich and famous, a dream he quickly achieved with huge success as a singer from the age of 17. In 1950 he was voted Singer of the Year, rivalling Bing Crosby.

Without much passion, and in a bid to promote his career, he married the famous actress Debbie Reynolds, with whom he had two children. The marriage was not particularly happy and Eddie preferred the company of his best friend Mike Todd, on whom he modelled himself. From Mike he learned how to spend and how to live like a prince to prove his star status. Eddie partied, drank and wanted to flaunt his success while Debbie, raised in a Christian fundamentalist family, was a thrifty stay-at-home, not a woman of the world.

To make matters worse, Eddie made use of the services of a certain Max Jacobson. Better-known as 'Dr Feelgood', Max was a 'doctor' who haunted the studios and prescribed 'vitamin cocktails' to his patients. His 'cocktails' were laced with amphetamine to give his patients energy. Such drugs were unlegislated in the 1950s and little was known about their effects. Since 1953 Eddie had been having injections of these mysterious miracle drugs, later learning how to inject himself. While these amphetamines initially had a euphoric effect, they soon gave way to devastating downers. Eddie grew dependent, needed larger and larger dosages and suffered terrible depressions when the drugs had less effect. The amphetamines made it possible to survive on very little sleep but it is not difficult to imagine the effects of such a regime on body and mind. By 1958, when he threw himself wholeheartedly into his new relationship with Elizabeth, Eddie was completely addicted – and he quickly became addicted to the violet-eyed Elizabeth.

Based on loss and despair, such a union was bound to be ill-fated. Eddie ended his four-year marriage with Debbie Reynolds and replaced his friend Mike Todd in the still-warm bed of Elizabeth Taylor. Journalists were quick to accuse Elizabeth of being a 'husband-stealer' and reminded the public that Eddie and pretty Debbie had two children, aged one and two. The League of Decency urged boycotts of Fisher's records and Taylor's films. But Elizabeth was unmoved, snapping at a journalist during an interview, 'What do you expect me to do? Sleep alone?' She topped this by echoing a tirade from *Cat on a Hot Tin Roof*, 'Mike is dead and I'm alive.' Eager to be outraged, the public found it hard to forgive the woman whose image henceforward was that of a dangerous home-breaker. Elizabeth received tons of hate mail while the press fed off the situation. Richard Brooks maintained that but for this inopportune scandal Elizabeth would certainly have won an Oscar for *Cat on a Hot Tin Roof*.

In early 1959 it was rumoured that Elizabeth Taylor was suffering from deep depression and had to be hospitalized in a Kansas clinic. To scotch the rumours, she immediately dined out with Eddie at a popular restaurant, inviting the whole of the press corps to join them with champagne for all. During this new, euphoric period, Elizabeth quickly regained weight and once more the press seized on it. 'Liz Taylor is putting on too much weight' headlined *Photoplay*.

Like Mike Todd, Eddie was Jewish. Elizabeth now decided to convert to Judaism. During the ceremony she was given the Hebrew name 'Elisheba Rachel' and the rabbi assured her 'with this name as a pledge, you are now part of the House of Israel and you assume all its rights, privileges and responsibilities'. When Elizabeth made a donation to the State of Israel, repercussions in the Arab world quickly followed. Ironically, although she was preparing to play the

Egyptian queen Cleopatra on the screen, her films were censored in Egypt and the Arab League forbade them to be shown in the Arab countries of Africa and the Middle East.

Elizabeth installed herself in a luxury villa near Las Vegas, where Eddie was appearing for a month at the Tropicana Hotel. His divorce was about to come through and they decided to get married immediately. The ceremony took place in a Las Vegas synagogue At 27, Elizabeth had celebrated her fourth wedding – and of course it would not be the last.

The honeymoon was spent in Europe, where Elizabeth was filming *Suddenly, Last Summer* in London. It was her second consecutive film based on a Tennessee Williams play and her first to be directed by the great Joseph L. Mankiewicz. When she arrived on set, the director was blunt: 'Are you planning on losing any weight?' he asked. 'I think maybe you should do a little toning up [Spoto].' Elizabeth, who realised that once again she had taken too much of a good thing, immediately went on a diet and managed to lose ten kilos (22 lbs).

With a screenplay jointly written by Tennessee Williams and Gore Vidal, *Suddenly, Last Summer* starred Elizabeth, her friend Montgomery Clift and the great Katharine Hepburn. But the atmosphere on set was tense: Montgomery Clift was by now hopelessly addicted to alcohol and drugs, Tennessee Williams was rarely sober and Katharine Hepburn was worried about the ailing Spencer Tracy. Affronted by the attacks of the British press, Elizabeth insisted that journalists should be banned from the set. She had to deliver long, poetic monologues and gave a stunning performance. A long 12-page tirade took two whole days to film, after which she was utterly exhausted and had to spend two days in bed. As usual, she entered completely into her character, to the extent that after her last monologue she broke down in tears on the set. Although still young, she had known suffering, widowhood, what Tennessee Williams called 'life's monstrosity' and from now on could create on screen deeply tortured characters devastated by the brutality of existence. She described the making of this film as the most testing but also the most stimulating experience of her career. Although her performance was certainly worthy of a third Academy Award nomination, the much-desired Oscar eluded her; in 1959 however, she was hailed by the press as the 'fifth American actress'.

While Eddie remained madly in love with Elizabeth, he was finding it increasingly difficult to handle the media pressure on their relationship. On her part, Elizabeth still felt married to Mike and always wore his ring. 'I never took it off,' she said. 'If I couldn't wear it in a film I'd pin it to my underwear.' [Spoto] The amphetamine-dependent Eddie drank and gambled large sums at Hollywood's gaming tables. Elizabeth had become a huge star while her husband was nothing more than his wife's shadow. As if to prove it, the couple began a search for blame; once again, it was the end of the beginning.

Around this time, Elizabeth was offered the part of Cleopatra in a big-budget movie. The role seemed perfect. Like Cleopatra, Elizabeth was a powerful woman who had learned never to give up; she went into battle and negotiated for herself the biggest deal in movie history.

When producer Walter Wanger called to ask if she would accept the part, she said that she would do it for a salary of one million dollars. This was an unheard-of price in those days; neither Marilyn Monroe nor Audrey Hepburn got paid that much. The Fox executives decided to look for another actress, which spurred Elizabeth to reconsider her demands. Still bargaining hard, she

declared that she would now play the queen of Egypt 'for a minimum guarantee of $750,000 plus ten per cent of the gross'. A signing was staged for the press, although a real contract would not be ready for almost a year since Elizabeth, the experienced businesswoman, was still in negotiation.

In the meantime, MGM cast her in *Butterfield 8,* adapted from John O'Hara's dark novel, in which she would play the role of a high-class call girl. She did not want to take the part, protesting that 'I've been here for 17 years and I was never asked to play such a horrible role as Gloria Wandrous. She's a sick nymphomaniac. I won't do it for anything.' [Spoto] But she had no choice and, while she detested the screenplay and her character, ironically, she earned her first Oscar for this film.

On 28 July 1960, Elizabeth finally signed her contract for Cleopatra. It was a deal without precedent: she would be paid $125,000 per week for 16 weeks ($400,000 in total), $50,000 per week after 16 weeks, 10 per cent of the film's gross receipts and various professional expenses to enable her to live like a queen throughout filming. Never had an actress exacted such a salary. 'She stands to make two or three million dollars from this!' noted Wanger. Not quite: when filming ended Elizabeth had pocketed more than $7,000,000.

Shooting started in Pinewood Studios, near London, at the end of September. The parts of Caesar and Mark Antony went to Peter Finch and Stephen Boyd. Thousands of extras were hired and set expenses were colossal. But the screenplay underwent constant modification, the weather was disastrous and Elizabeth did not feel very well. In fact, everything went wrong from the very beginning. Despite a week off, Elizabeth's health did not seem to improve; the Queen's doctor was called in and he diagnosed that her fever and headaches were caused by a dental abscess. Her condition worsened and the tooth was extracted, delaying filming for another week. Finally, when studio executives saw the first rushes, they demanded that the director be replaced. Filming was halted for another week and the producers tore their hair out. They had already lost $2 million and discussed replacing their star with another more tractable, healthier actress. In January, after three months of wasted shooting, Mankiewicz took over as director. None of the earlier scenes could be used and he decided to rewrite the script totally.

In January 1961, everything began again from the beginning, but the production's bad luck was not yet over. On returning to London after a holiday in Palm Springs, Elizabeth fell ill again, coming down with viral pneumonia contracted in the draughty London studios. Her condition worsened and she was taken to the London Clinic, where her doctor explained that if she had not had a tracheotomy, 'she might have survived 15 minutes longer, but no more'. She slipped into a coma and news bulletins announced that she was dying. Journalists braced themselves for the death of Elizabeth Taylor and one press agency even announced her death.

Clearly no one reckoned with Elizabeth's will to live and in March she began to recover. A few months later she reflected on this difficult experience: 'I knew I was going to die. When I regained consciousness, the one thing I wanted to know was if I were going to die, and when, but I couldn't make myself heard. Only I heard myself calling out, begging God to help me. I was afraid. I was angry. I didn't want to die. I came to, then slipped back into nothingness. I stopped breathing four times, I died four times. I felt as if I were going, falling into a horrible black void. I felt my skin coming away. But even when I was in a coma I still kept my hands balled into fists, the doctor told me later. He said that I lived because I'd struggled so hard to survive.'

Indeed, the fact that Elizabeth did not die had a positive effect in regaining public sympathy, to the extent that when she left hospital she was mobbed by fans who almost wrenched the door off her Rolls-Royce. Now she had almost the status of a goddess-actress, a role that corresponded rather well with the character she was about to play on screen.

By now Fox's losses on this ill-fated movie amounted to $7 million but there was no going back. The London shoot seemed to be doomed; the $600,000 sets were demolished and the production was transferred to Rome, where it was hoped the climate would be more favourable. Peter Finch and Stephen Richard Boyd were paid off; Rex Harrison was hired to play Caesar and Richard Burton was cast as Mark Antony.

Born in 1925, Richard Burton was the twelfth of thirteen children from an impoverished Welsh family. Like his brothers he was destined to become a miner until it was noticed that he had an exceptional voice and extraordinary charisma. Recognizing his talent, one of his teachers took him into his home and trained him for a career on the stage. In gratitude, Richard adopted the surname of his mentor, Philip Burton, to emphasize the fact that from now on his life would never be the same. His father had been an alcoholic and Richard swore he would never drink – a promise he did not manage to keep for long. At first, he played small parts but by 22 he was beginning to make his name in Shakespeare, playing Hamlet, Othello and Prince Hal. In 1951 he married Sybil Williams, who was his greatest support during the following 12 years. His career was dazzling and he was hailed as one of the great Shakespearean actors. Despite being married, he was a well-known seducer although he later said 'I couldn't be unfaithful to my wife without feeling a profound sense of guilt.' [Spoto] He was drawn to Hollywood for the money, as he later declared many times, 'My decision to do *Cleopatra* was prompted by laziness and cupidity.' His love-affair with Elizabeth Taylor would prove to be one of the most beautiful but also most intense and violent romances in cinema history.

While waiting for *Cleopatra* to start shooting in Italy, Elizabeth passed the spring in Beverly Hills, where she slowly recovered from her medical setbacks; she also lost 8 kilos (17½ lbs), indicating that she was at last positive about making the film.

Meanwhile Mankiewicz toiled on the screenplay of *Cleopatra*. Every day he rewrote drafts provided by Lawrence Durrell, Sydney Buchman and Ronald MacDougall, trying to give more depth and character to his female lead. Elizabeth felt herself more than ever invested with a mission; she saw herself as an emissary of peace in a discordant world and she again went to Moscow. She also decided to adopt a child with Eddie Fisher and placed an advertisement in a German magazine. She was immediately offered a six-month old girl and in September 1961 Elizabeth asked her secretary to fly over to view the infant. Little Petra Heisig was undernourished, had serious health problems and was congenitally deformed. The same day Elizabeth began filming *Cleopatra* in Rome; rising to the occasion, she ignored the bad news about the child and flew to Germany where she signed the official papers to enable her to start the adoption process. The child was transferred to one of the best clinics in Switzerland to plan for the operations she would shortly require. Petra, renamed Maria, arrived at the Fisher's home in Rome on Christmas Day.

The new Cleopatra set, one hour from Rome, was gigantic. The scenes in the Forum were shot at Cinecittà and those of Alexandria by the seaside at a private beach in Torre Astura, Anzio. But when filming commenced in September 1961 it appeared that Mankiewicz had written only half the screenplay; he had to shoot by day and write at night, as he explained, 'I awoke at five-thirty or six and gulped down a Dexedrine.' [Spoto] Like Eddie and so many others, he needed to take amphetamines just to function and get through another day of drudgery: 'I was given a shot after lunch to keep me going through the afternoon. Then I was given a shot after dinner so I could write until two in the morning, and then I got a final shot at two so I could go to sleep.' [Spoto] Every morning it took two hours to apply the Cleopatra makeup.

At last, in February 1962, Elizabeth Taylor and Richard Burton filmed their first scene together. According to Richard, the experienced seducer, he was not initially impressed. 'All this stuff about Elizabeth being the most beautiful woman in the world is absolute nonsense. She's a pretty girl, of course, and she has wonderful eyes. But she has a double chin and an overdeveloped chest and she's rather short in the leg [from here on, all unattributed quotes are courtesy of Spoto]

At first the two stars communicated through other people: Burton called her 'Miss Tits' to which Taylor retorted that she was the one leading lady Richard Burton wasn't going to get. But, as in the movies, the apparent indifference and insults quickly turned into savage passion. The two stars began to meet frequently, each intrigued and attracted to the other. Richard was fascinated by Elizabeth's arrogance, vulgarity and her wild side, while she was enthralled by his deep voice, his passion, his Shakespearean experience and his great literary knowledge – it was said he could recite Shakespeare backwards as a party trick. The two started having lunch together, drinking numerous bottles of wine during their lengthy meals.

At first Elizabeth was taken aback by the Welsh actor's neediness and excesses. She recalled how, on their first day's filming, Richard had such a ferocious hangover he could hardly drink his coffee and she had to help him bring the cup to his lips. 'That just endeared him so to me ... My heart just went out to him.' With Richard, Elizabeth rediscovered what she had experienced with her first husband and also with Mike Todd: the two brawlers squabbled, drank too much, flew at each other and slugged it out before making-up. When he drank, Richard lost all control and beat up his lover; the following morning Elizabeth would have a black eye or a split lip. Rex Harrison recalled how 'at the height of it, Elizabeth and Richard kept hitting at each other and giving each other black eyes and not turning up at the studio'. But this fierce passion undoubtedly had the effect of generating real emotion on the set and it's said that the couple's clinches continued long after the cameras had stopped turning.

It didn't take long for the press to get wind of this new liaison, to the dismay of Eddie Fisher who took off in a rage for Switzerland and then Portugal. Although she had already lived through many similar scenarios, Sybil, Burton's wife, was equally devastated by the news and prepared to leave for New York.

Even though she was still married, Elizabeth was now intent on wedding Richard, but he was more realistic and retorted that his wife would never accept a divorce. He even told her, after a month of frenetic passion, that it was now time for them to stop playing games and to return to their respective spouses. Elizabeth panicked; in desperation that evening she swallowed a large quantity of sleeping pills. Discovered in time, she was rushed to hospital; the studio hushed up rumours of suicide and gave out that she had food poisoning.

On 27 February 1962 Elizabeth celebrated her 30th birthday. Eddie returned from his travels and tried to recover his wife's affection by giving her an expensive diamond ring and organizing a big party in a famous Roman nightclub. Flattered, no doubt, Elizabeth continued to live with her husband but she was more than ever madly in love with Richard Burton, from whom she demanded a love token in the form of a brooch worth the modest sum of $150,000.

Elizabeth, queen of Egypt and Hollywood

At some point in mid-March 1962, Richard joined Elizabeth and Eddie for dinner. The uneasy trio had a lot to drink and Richard dramatically asked Elizabeth who she loved: him or her husband. Elizabeth did not answer and he repeated his question loudly. 'You', she said. Much smaller and half Burton's weight – Richard was 1.93m tall (6ft 4in) and weighted 95 kilos (209lbs) – the humiliated Eddie Fisher crumbled and left Italy, checking himself into a New York hospital a week later. The tragedy continued and Elizabeth now had high hopes of obtaining a divorce.

The adulterous couple's scandalous life dominated the headlines and even provoked a serious Congressional debate in Washington, where Elizabeth was accused of disrespect 'to the national flag and the nation'. A member of the House of Representatives named Iris Blitch declared 'I hope that the Attorney General, in the name of American womanhood, will take the necessary measures to determine whether or not Miss Taylor and Mr Burton are ineligible for re-entry into the United States on the grounds of undesirability'. The conservative press and various lobbies accused the couple of being responsible for 'moral decadence'.

In early summer 1962, the turbulent filming of *Cleopatra* came to an end. Mankiewicz wanted the final film to run for seven hours and to be shown in two parts, but the studio refused and cut it, so that the final version ran to 'a mere' four hours. The director was furious and tried to have his name removed from the credits. Although the film was very poorly received, it was an undoubted masterpiece, in which Elizabeth Taylor's acting was more convincing than ever.

For the next two years Elizabeth and Richard continued their relationship without worrying about what America's moral majority might think. After all, this was 1962 and morals had begun to change. They drank, fought and hid nothing from the media. Taylor and Burton epitomized that lust for life that began with James Dean and Elvis Presley and was characteristic of the winds of revolt, excess and freedom that now blew across a repressed and constrained America. 'Even our fights are fun', Elizabeth later wrote. 'Our fights are delightful screaming matches, and Richard is rather like a small atom bomb going off – sparks fly, walls shake, floors vibrate.' [Taraborelli] The couple unleashed a savage, Dionysian force, erasing the past and seeming to announce a new Hollywood era.

In reality, Richard was finding it difficult to control his alcoholism. His habit was to begin the day with five or six Bloody Marys and to drink uncontrollably from lunchtime, during which he was capable of knocking back several bottles. As his brother said, 'To be in his company was to play life dangerously; the fun times were interrupted by terrifying bouts of depression and ill temper when he became a stranger to us all. No one could tell when the storms would break.'

Bouts of depression that the actor liked to call, poetically, his 'Welsh moments'. To make things worse Elizabeth, who had a remarkable tolerance for alcohol, also began to follow this punishing regime that did not bode well for the long term.

Despite their torrid encounters, Richard continued seeing his wife, even telling journalists that he had no intention of marrying Elizabeth. After *Cleopatra*, Elizabeth and Richard signed to make a movie together in London in which Richard played, appropriately enough, an alcoholic husband. (Orson Welles also had a role in the movie.) *The VIPs*, took less than a month to film and Elizabeth collected one million dollars while Richard got $500,000. In addition, both stars got 20 per cent of the gross, which totalled $14 million, giving them a remuneration unprecedented at the time. Thanks to the Taylor–Burton relationship, the movie industry was now entering a new era.

In 1963 Richard played the title role in *Becket* while Elizabeth fronted 'Elizabeth Taylor's London', a guided tour of London made for television, for which she again collected a handsome fee. In fact she had nothing more interesting to do and next accompanied Richard to Mexico, where he was to make *The Night of the Iguana,* directed by John Huston from a play by Tennessee Williams.

The film was to be shot on the wild Pacific coastline, which was accessible only by boat. The famously eccentric Huston loved strained and conflicted situations and, true to form, he provoked his cast and enjoyed stirring things up. On the first day of filming he presented each of the company (Richard Burton, Ava Gardner, Deborah Kerr and Sue Lyon plus Elizabeth Taylor) with a gold-plated Derringer pistol and a gold bullet engraved with the actor's name, asking with a smile which of them would be first to resort to violence. 'It was like being in an Agatha Christie thriller', commented Deborah Kerr. The atmosphere in this isolated setting, in humid topical conditions, promised to be difficult.

That autumn of 1963, Elizabeth devoted herself to her three children, who had accompanied her to Mexico, and to Richard. She would arrive on set every morning at 10am, immediately ordering vodka and lemon or a vodka martini for herself before moving on to tequila. In his diary John Huston described her as wearing a simple 'bikini, under a green and white Mexican tunic ... her figure had disappeared under enormous rolls of flesh'. Huston's assistant gave her own account of the actress's provocative attire: 'Elizabeth arrived on the set wearing a loose top and bikini bottom of sheer white batiste trimmed with red embroidery. She had no bra on and you literally could see the complete upper structure. Imposing.' [Kelley]

In this sweaty, torrid ambiance Taylor and Burton drank more and more and when Richard was drunk he insulted and humiliated his companion, accusing her of having put on weight and inferring that she didn't have the intellect to measure up to him. In front of friends, for example, he would call Elizabeth 'Miss Tits', 'Monkey boobs', 'Fatty' or even 'Big Hollywood baby', to which Elizabeth tactfully responded with 'Shut up' before riposting with 'Lush'. And so the game continued, in effect to the tune of *Je t'aime, moi non plus.* 'Before meeting Elizabeth, I didn't know what total love was', explained Burton later.

'The only problem was she also wanted my soul, and I wanted to stay free.' Thus were laid down the sado-masochistic encounters that would be so well-developed in *Who's afraid of Virginia Woolf?* As Richard said, a little later, 'Our way of life was a first-class recipe for organized suicide.'

In this atmosphere worthy of Malcolm Lowry's *Under the Volcano,* the couple decided to buy an enormous villa in Puerto Vallarta, Mexico. Sybil Burton finally agreed to divorce Richard, charging him with 'abandonment and cruel and inhuman treatment'. On 14 January 1964 Elizabeth in turn filed for divorce, accusing Eddie Fisher of having abandoned her in March 1962. She also obtained custody of the child Maria, who later took Burton's name.

Elizabeth and Richard spent Christmas with their families before flying to Los Angeles to be greeted by a hysterical crowd. They stayed briefly in the presidential suite of the Beverly Wilshire Hotel before leaving for Toronto, where Richard was to return to the stage in the role of Hamlet. Elizabeth would not work for another year, just to be with Richard who was, despite everything, becoming a major international star.

On 15 March 1964, after two years of living together, they were finally married in Montreal in a Unitarian ceremony that took place in a suite at the Ritz-Carlton Hotel. Richard was 38 and Elizabeth 32. It was her fifth marriage. Of course she arrived late for the ceremony, prompting her future spouse to mutter 'Isn't that fat little tart here yet? She'll be late for the Last bloody Judgement.' When she finally arrived, Elizabeth responded with typical nonchalance. 'I don't know why he's so nervous. We've been sleeping together for two years.' It was in the same vein of corrosive humour that Richard summer up his wife's marriages: 'Her first marriage was a complete mistake. Her second was handicapped by an enormous difference in ages. Her third was perfect, but the husband is dead. The fourth is deplorable. As for the fifth – that's me – let's hope it won't be [deplorable].'

And so began ten long years of passion, wandering and mental torture.

Chaos, self-destruction and diamonds

The private life of Taylor and Burton was practically nonexistent: everything they did together was done under media scrutiny; they were dogged by photographers, cameras and microphones. Such pressure is hard to tolerate and it pushed the couple into heavy drinking. During the run of *Hamlet* in Boston, Elizabeth's hair was torn out and her back and arms bruised by delirious crowds. She was so upset by the scene that doctors sedated her on the spot, thinking she was in danger of death.

It was probably for fiscal rather than sentimental reasons that she renounced her American citizenship, although she said, 'It's not that I love America less, but I love my husband more.' It was another insult to her conservative American public, who already had difficulty in pardoning her amorous adventures. During this time she continued to overeat and to gain weight, justifying herself humorously to the press, 'If I get fat enough, they will not ask me to do any more films.

Elizabeth and Richard agreed to co-star in *The Sandpiper,* directed by Vicente Minnelli. As in *The Night of the Iguana,* Richard Burton played a defrocked clergyman. Unfortunately, despite the excellent casting and a major director,

the result was barely convincing. No matter. Elizabeth pocketed her usual million dollars and Richard his half-million, as he would from now on. 'For the money, we will dance,' commented the cynical Burton.

The positive side of this depressing experience was that while filming, Elizabeth and Richard met Ernest Lehman, one of Hollywood's best scriptwriters (noted for the screenplay for *North by Northwest*). Lehman told them he had just seen a play by Edward Albee called *Who's Afraid of Virginia Woolf?* and had been deeply moved. Why not try adapting it for the screen? It was a daring idea that would soon bear fruit.

To play Martha the 33-year-old Elizabeth had to age by 15 years and gain 12 kilos (25 lbs) to 'get inside' her character. Richard would be perfect in the role of George, a pontificating university professor, like him a complete alcoholic. Elizabeth would be paid $1.1 million with, of course, a percentage of the gross receipts.

Yet, once again, Elizabeth was hit with a run of bad luck. While she was in Paris, her favourite jewels, valued at £17,000 were stolen from her hotel. She then flew to Dublin where she was in her car when her chauffeur ran over and killed a pedestrian. Richard, after a relatively long period of sobriety, began drinking again and when she learned that her father had suffered a cerebral haemorrhage Elizabeth rushed to be with him in Los Angeles.

When *Who's Afraid of Woolf?* opened it drew raves from the critics and was nominated for six Academy Awards. Elizabeth took the Oscar for Best Actress, making this her second – and last –acknowledgement from the Academy. The role of Martha had certainly been one of the most ambitious and hardest for her to create, as director Mike Nichols explained: 'She had painful things to do. She had to spit in Richard's face, take after take after take. He didn't mind but she finally became very upset. On a piece like this something bad has to come out of everyone, but I'd say it came out of Elizabeth only once. It was anger.' [Kelley] In this intense and stormy movie Elizabeth gave proof of incomparable maturity and undoubtedly played her best role. She probably realized that she had been offered the greatest screenplay of her career and she gave herself to it, body and soul. As a goddess of the cinema, at the age of 34 the star was now at the peak of the Hollywood pantheon and, alas, never managed to go higher.

In early 1966 Elizabeth and Richard went to Oxford to act together in *Doctor Faustus,* Christopher Marlowe's famous play, which was later adapted for the cinema. In 1967 they co-starred in *The Taming of the Shrew,* a film which unfortunately revealed more than it concealed. Thinking themselves on a roll, they signed to film *The Comedians,* based on a screenplay by the great writer Graham Greene.

Suddenly Elizabeth learned of the death of her close friend Montgomery Clift, who had just turned 45. She was in shock and his death left a great emptiness in her life although she nevertheless continued making a series of films. It might have been expected that *Reflections in a Golden Eye* (1967), adapted from Carson McCullers' bestseller and directed at Cinecittà by John Huston, co-starring Marlon Brando, would draw acclaim from the public and the critics. But it bombed. And while Tennessee Williams himself wrote the screenplay for *Boom!* (1968), this collaboration between Elizabeth and Richard once again proved mediocre.

During this period, Elizabeth distanced herself increasingly from her children who were essentially brought up by an army of nannies, tutors and servants.

She was drinking too much and it began to show. Despite her protestations the queen of Hollywood was scared of ageing and to obliterate this angst she consumed, shopped and spent extravagantly. In less than ten years, the Burtons blazed through $65 million but their business interests prospered and Elizabeth and Richard transformed themselves into a conquering empire, setting up a company called Taybur (*Taylor-Burton*). Taybur invested in luxury Parisian boutiques and in real estate all over the world. They also bought Rolls-Royces and paintings by Rembrandt, Van Gogh, Picasso, Monet and Utrillo – whatever might be good-value investments. In addition they acquired a luxury yacht, a private plane and a helicopter. Richard covered his goddess in diamonds and furs, presenting her, for instance, with a Cartier diamond. It was the world's biggest diamond bought by an individual, but 'It's a troublesome stone,' Elizabeth would explain with some pride. 'I can't wear it without two security guards.' This was a condition of her insurance, itself prohibitive.

Press and public accused the Burtons of indecent and vulgar behaviour, to which Elizabeth retorted, 'I know I'm vulgar, but would you have me any other way?' While she and her husband had become seriously rich, they continued to get several million dollars per film. But was the Taylor–Burton empire strong? It seems that, just as in *Who's Afraid of Virginia Woolf?*, the crumbling partnership was teetering on the edge of an empire in decline.

Secret Ceremony (1968), in which Elizabeth starred with Mia Farrow, and its successor *The Only Game in Town*, with Warren Beatty, were both unremarkable. Elizabeth's feelings of disaffection were heightened when she underwent a hysterectomy following severe abdominal pain. Serious complications ensued and Richard heard her screaming in agony. Her convalescence was prolonged and she fell into a serious depression. At only 36 Elizabeth suddenly felt very old. Once again she had gained a lot of weight and now suffered from terrible sciatica. The vicious circle continued as she was prescribed heavy sedatives on which she quickly became dependent. Although she tried to cut down she soon moved on to massive doses and more potent painkillers.

In November 1968, Elizabeth was in Paris when she learned that her father had died in his sleep at home in Los Angeles. She flew home to attend the funeral, returning to Paris six days later. She had never felt close to her father and did not seem to be deeply affected by this loss. A few months later she learned of the death of her first husband, Nicky Hilton – the Grim Reaper was at large, awakening her worst nightmares. Drug-dependent and alcoholic, she became increasingly ill. Richard Burton, who seemed able to manage his dependence rather better than his wife, later said 'She always had a glass in her hand. I dreaded the moment when she would fall into a semi-conscious state after her evening injection.' In deep depression, Elizabeth had lost her zest for life and no longer had any interest in anything – not the cinema, not her husband and not her children.

In early 1969, she entered a clinic for the first time, in an effort to withdraw from her drug dependency. Her medical examination indicated that her liver was in poor condition. Richard wrote in his diary that she got drunk every evening, to the point of being 'stoned, unfocussed, unable to walk straight, talking in a slow, meaningless baby voice utterly without reason, like a demented child.' When she left the clinic in March she and Richard went to their Mexican villa, where the children came to visit them from Hawaii. The atmosphere was strained:

the Burtons were permanently intoxicated and passed their time bickering; in full adolescent revolt, the youngsters thought them 'pathetic' and spent most of their time in their bedrooms watching TV.

Between Richard and Elizabeth, as with George and Martha, it was war. When Richard told visitors that his wife could not live without alcohol, she retorted violently 'I want only one thing – for you to get out of my life.' Elizabeth's relationship with her mother was also strained and their conversations inevitably degenerated into squabbles. At the beginning of 1970, Elizabeth underwent an operation for haemorrhoids but complications sent her back to painkillers and once again she fell into dependency. During this period, however, Richard accomplished a miracle, not drinking a drop of alcohol for 140 days.

In October Michael, Elizabeth's 17-year-old son, got married in London. His mother came to the wedding and gave the young couple a Jaguar and a house. In early 1971 she started shooting *Zee & Company*, one of her worst films. A few months later, she learned that she was a grandmother at the age of 39. When Elizabeth visited her granddaughter in London, in the house she had given to her son and her daughter-in-law, she saw that it had been turned into a hippie commune. Michael, who had grown up accustomed to luxury and his mother's indifference, had completely rebelled against her material values. As he said, 'Mother's life seems just as fantastic to me as it must to everyone else. I really don't want any part of it. I just don't dig all those diamonds and things.' Naturally the son who completely rejected his mother chose to invert her values by adopting a counterculture philosophy. He played in a rock band and was later arrested by the police for growing marijuana in his home.

Sadly, Elizabeth now appeared in flop after flop. In 1972, she celebrated her 40th birthday, organizing with her husband's assistance a gigantic party at a hotel in Budapest, where Richard was filming *Bluebeard*. Among others, they invited Michael Caine, Ringo Starr and Princess Grace of Monaco. While Richard tried to stay sober and drank only water that evening, this respite would not endure. He soon relapsed spectacularly, drinking up to three bottles of vodka a day and becoming a complete wreck. This did not, however, prevent him from seducing – like the character he played – all the young actresses who starred with him. As the director of *Bluebeard* explained, filming was a real nightmare: 'Richard was drunk every evening when he left the studio, but he was also almost always drunk when he arrived in the morning … Despite this, all his co-stars were in love with him – with the exception of Virna Lisi – and when Elizabeth left Budapest, he didn't neglect them.' TV personality David Frost came to Budapest to interview the Burtons for his American talk show. During the two-hour interview, millions of TV viewers saw on their screens the pathetic spectacle of two completely drunk people slumped in their chairs, stumbling and slurring their speech.

This self-destructive phase did not prevent Elizabeth from making a series of insipid movies: *Zee & Co* (1972), *Hammersmith is Out* (1972), *Night Watch* (1973), *Ash Wednesday* (1973) and *Divorce His, Divorce Hers,* a terrible made-for-television movie. To make things worse, Richard who had (surprisingly) remained faithful during the ten chaotic years of their partnership, decided to spend a romantic weekend with a beautiful young actress he had met on the set of *Bluebeard*. Of this critical period in their marriage, he later said, 'Once I started being attracted to other women, I knew the game was up.' Outraged,

Elizabeth flew to Rome, where she met up with her friend Aristotle Onassis. That evening she telephoned her husband and ordered him to 'get that woman out of my bed!'

The pair reunited while stoically pursuing their 'total war', until the day in Rome when, after yet another row, Richard asked his wife to leave: 'I told her to get out, and to my surprise, she went. I couldn't believe it! I thought she would be back next day, but not a bit of it.' After ten years of destruction and self-destruction, Elizabeth was ready to throw in the towel. Naturally, she immediately found another man with whom she fell 'in love'. Henry Wynberg was a slick used-car salesman, ready to dance and party with her all night long. 'I've been totally dependent on love,' she confided to a journalist. But what does 'love' mean in this context? 'Passion', as she intended to imply, or unconditional love between two people, inevitably leading to destruction? Be that as it may, Elizabeth now issued a press release announcing her separation: 'I am convinced it would be a good and constructive idea if Richard and I separated for a while. Maybe we loved each other too much.'

In the same year, 1973, Elizabeth returned to Rome to make *The Driver's Seat*, another dreadful film, as she realized: 'We are shooting it differently, without a proper script.' Richard was also in Rome, making *The Journey*, directed by Vittorio de Sica. His co-star was the beautiful Sophia Loren, which did not fail to drive Elizabeth mad with rage. Despite the fact that her new companion, Henry Wynberg, was in attendance in Rome, Elizabeth saw the New Year in with Richard and announced that they were reconciled. The hellish saga continued as the couple holidayed in Mexico and celebrated their tenth wedding anniversary in rural northern California, where Richard was filming *The Klansman* with Lee Marvin, another inveterate drinker. Gallons of vodka were imbibed, with Elizabeth often trying to keep pace. The bickering and insults began again – everything was back to normal – until Richard had a fling with an 18-year-old and then with a married woman.

This time, enough was enough. Elizabeth packed her bags and flew to Los Angeles where she reunited with Henry Wynberg, always available when she needed him. Meanwhile, Richard had been rushed to hospital, where doctors told him that his liver and kidneys were utterly wrecked and that unless he stopped drinking he would be dead in less than six months. Richard, as was his nature, did not take them seriously; he carried on as usual, not dying until ten years year.

In April 1974, the Burton's lawyer announced to the international press that the couple had decided to initiate divorce proceedings, ending their ten years of marriage. Two months later the divorce became official.

The decline of the Elizabethan empire

At this point, a film of Elizabeth Taylor's life might be entitled *Four Divorces and a Funeral*: at 42, she was the widow of Mike Todd and had divorced Nicky Hilton, Michael Wilding, Eddie Fisher and now Richard Burton.

From 1975, Henry Wynberg faded into the background. Elizabeth was still obsessed with her ex-husband, as Burton himself testified: 'Twenty minutes after our divorce, she phoned me and asked, "Richard, do you think we did the right thing?"' In fact Wynberg was hardly suited to the role of Prince Charming:

this small-time businessman was now indicted for fraud, having turned back the odometers on four cars he had sold, and was sentenced to three years on probation. Nevertheless he accompanied Elizabeth to Russia where she was to film *The Scarlet Empress*, with Jane Fonda, directed by George Cukor. In Moscow she came down with 'flu and then contracted dysentery. When filming finished in August she received a telegram from Richard, asking her to join him in Gstaad, Switzerland, 'for a serious discussion'. Without hesitation she left for Switzerland, accompanied by the trusty Wynberg, who would rapidly be dismissed. Richard had temporarily stopped drinking, although this state of sobriety clearly would not last.

A few days later, Elizabeth and Richard announced that they could not keep apart from each other and that they had decided to remarry. The couple immediately recommenced their travels around the world, visiting South Africa, Italy and Israel before ending up in Botswana, where they married. It was Elizabeth's sixth wedding, to her fifth husband. That evening Richard began drinking again, as if to confirm that the dream would not last long.

In November the couple flew to London, where Richard celebrated his 50th birthday. Guests were surprised to see that he was again on the wagon. Elizabeth was not feeling well and entered a London clinic for physiotherapy on her back. The sado-masochistic habits quickly returned: Richard had a fling with a tall, blonde English model; Elizabeth retaliated by picking up a man she met in a discotheque, one Peter Darmanin, on whom she took out her anger with insults and blows, leaving a scar over his eyebrow. One month on, when he was bitten by one of his mistress's dogs, he realized it was time to pack his bags before the situation degenerated further. As he told a journalist, 'Romance with Elizabeth! Man, it isn't easy!' Back in California, Elizabeth returned to her faithful Wynberg, with whom she celebrated her 44th birthday. But this relationship soon ended – while still on probation Wynberg had become implicated in a sordid paedophiliac affair and was accused of providing drugs and alcohol to four teenage girls, with having had sex with them, and of having photographed them in compromising positions.

Spring 1976 saw Elizabeth continuing her life of luxury and debauch, attending every party to which she was invited. During one of these evenings in a trendy nightclub she met Iranian Ambassador Ardeshir Zahedi, with whom she continued her bacchanalian evening. Between heedlessness and despair, she gained so much weight that she became obese. On 29 July the lawyer acting for both Elizabeth and Richard delivered the couple the official certificate of their new divorce, on which Elizabeth commented with some insight, 'I love Richard Burton with every fibre of my soul, but we can't be together. We're too mutually self-destructive.'

By now, however, she had already set her heart on John Warner, a right-wing, conservative politician. He was rich, authoritarian and respectable; in the eyes of Elizabeth he seemed, for the moment, to have every good quality.

If Hollywood had lost interest in the actress, she didn't care; she no longer needed it. When she first visited her new suitor's estate, a handsome farm in romantic South Virginia, she felt so peaceful that she saw herself in the new role of a housewife. Maybe she would learn to make apple-pie and look after John's children ... Perhaps she would manage to reduce her colossal consumption of gin, whisky and vodka ... Who knows, everything felt possible. John and Elizabeth married in Virginia on

4 December 1976 but the idyllic story of a beautiful princess renewed and restored by her Southern gentleman-farmer could not last. John became increasingly authoritarian and Elizabeth, living in the shadow of his political career, quickly felt stifled. Although she was neither a feminist nor a Marxist, Elizabeth had never been a right-wing extremist and hardly represented the Puritan values of good old upright, conservative America.

Now extremely overweight, Elizabeth was offered only small roles in mediocre made-for-television movies and it seemed preferable to remain cloistered in her Virginian farm, where she began to be seriously bored. The more so as, on 7 November 1978, John Warner, after a gruelling campaign during which his docile wife had to shake thousands of hands across the country, was finally elected to the US Senate. The ambitious husband now worked night and day and had no time to spare for his wife. It was clearly the beginning of the end.

Once again Elizabeth sank into depression: she overate, smoked a packet of cigarettes per day, drank all day and slept with the aid of massive doses of sedatives. Pursuing her self-destructive course, she drunkenly stumbled about her large mansion, often falling over and damaging herself, first a finger, then a rib, then her hip. In July 1979, Michael Wilding, the father of her two sons, died at the age of 67. Elizabeth flew to England to attend his funeral.

It was in this icy context that Elizabeth and John discussed the possibility of a friendly separation. Elizabeth was offered a part in *The Mirror Crack'd,* based on an Agatha Christie thriller; she would be appearing with her old friend Rock Hudson. The film was to be shot in England and the timing offered her a marvellous respite. Next she starred on Broadway in Lillian Hellman's play *The Little Foxes*, for a salary of $50,000 dollars a week, the largest ever paid to any stage actor. Audiences queued to see the living legend in the flesh but critics did not hold back, calling her the 'old galleon' or even 'Miss Piggy'.

In early 1981 Elizabeth bought an opulent villa in Bel Air, one of the smartest sections of Los Angeles. The queen installed herself in her chateau with her servants, her masterpieces, her projection-room and her swimming-pool, in a manner reminiscent of Gloria Swanson, the ageing queen of Hollywood's golden age in *Sunset Boulevard*. Elizabeth Taylor still lives at 700, Nimes Road, alone, surrounded by her animals, servants, trinkets and all her memories.

Alcoholic and drug-dependent, addicted to Percodan, the fallen star's situation worried her entourage. 'How long can she keep up this behaviour?' asked one of her friends. She herself admitted 'I reached a point where I would take one or two Percodan mixed with booze before I could go out in the evening and face people. I thought it would help me, because that combination would make me kind of talkative but it gave me false courage. I felt I was being charming. I was probably boring as hell. During the course of an evening – like every four hours – I'd take another two Percodan. And of course I had a hollow leg. I could drink anybody under the table and never get drunk.'

By the time her divorce from John Warner was pronounced on 5 November 1982, Elizabeth had already found a new suitor, Victor Luna, who accompanied her to Egypt, the Lebanon and Israel. In an echo of her trip to Moscow with Mike Todd, she announced that she had decided to embark on a 'diplomatic mission' to the Middle East, 'to try to create peace between Israel and the Lebanon'. She had no official backing and very nearly became an international joke.

On her return, she was invited to return to the stage, playing opposite her ex-husband Richard Burton in *Private Lives*. While the couple replenished their exchequers during the run, which lasted from April to November 1982, the two actors, soused in alcohol and rancour, both seemed to be teetering on the edge of a precipice.

Seized with abdominal pains, Elizabeth was hospitalized again, taking a bottle of Jack Daniels with her. Her friends descended to try to make her understand that this time the situation could not continue *she must look after herself*. They left her to reflect in her room for a good two hours and when they returned, Elizabeth finally faced up to the evidence and agreed to enter the Betty Ford Center. She spent seven long weeks in the famous detoxification clinic near Palm Springs, deprived of alcohol and drugs for the first time in 20 years. It was a difficult experience, as she wrote in a diary she kept at the time: 'I feel like hell. I'm going through withdrawal. My heart feels big and pounding. I can feel the blood rush through my body. I can almost see it, running like red water over the boulders in my pain-filled neck and shoulders, then through my ears and into my pounding head. My eyelids flutter. Oh, God, I am so, so tired.' For the first time in her life, the great star had to stop and take time to look inside herself, to undergo the painful work of introspection. As she said, 'Fame and the very nature of acting – it's schizophrenic. You become, in a role, somebody else. You're not yourself, but a character you portray.' This typifies the career of Elizabeth Taylor, and the way she had been damaged since her earliest years under the Hollywood spotlight: by creating her identity through the multiple personalities she incarnated on screen, she ended up believing that her life would unfold like a movie. Her existence had been transformed into fiction while her sense of self had disintegrated into multiple images disconnected from reality. At the age of 52, Elizabeth Taylor needed to redefine who she was and what she expected from life – apart from a collection of diamonds, pictures and men.

Intoxication and detox

On 20 January 1984, after seven gruelling weeks, Elizabeth left the Betty Ford Centre and was reunited with Victor Luna. Their wedding was planned for the spring and in the meantime the couple holidayed around the world. But on 5 August 1984, she learned that Richard Burton, the man who undoubtedly mattered most in her life, was dead. Only 58, he had succumbed to a cerebral haemorrhage. Victor Luna recalls how his fiancée became completely hysterical before fainting when she heard the news: 'She was completely out of control. I realized then how deeply tied she was to this man, how vital a role he had played in her life. And I realized I could never have that special place in her heart she keeps for Burton. For me, the romance was over, and I told Elizabeth that.'

She was deeply hurt when Sally, Burton's wife of one year, telephoned to ask her not to come to the funeral, which was held in Switzerland, although she could attend the memorial service for her ex-husband in Wales. In fact, Elizabeth attended only the London memorial service and on her return gave Victor Luna his engagement ring back. That autumn, however, she met a New York businessman, Dennis Stein, who shared her life for a time.

It was also in 1984 that she became friendly with Michael Jackson, then 26. The two stars had bonded immediately. He also declared that he considered

Elizabeth 'a mother, a friend. She is Mother Theresa, Princess Diana, the Queen of England and Wendy.'

Between 1985 and 1986, Elizabeth acted in several films (*Malice in Wonderland, North and South* and *There Must be a Pony*). In time she split up with Dennis Stein, once again returning an engagement ring and declaring that 'I almost made a mistake. I think maybe finally I'm growing up, and it's about time, too.' But she added 'No matter what happens, I'm loud, noisy and earthy and ready for much more living.' As she would later say, 'I couldn't live without love but I could have done without getting married.' Mischievous and incorrigible, she later declared with the mixture of plain-speaking and humour that sums up her complex personality: 'Marriage is like a restaurant meal: you don't know if you've made the right choice until you digest it.'

In 1985, it became known that Rock Hudson had contracted AIDS. Deeply shocked, Elizabeth began her campaign for AIDS research. It soon became her mission in life. She railed against the government, which at that time did practically nothing to develop research, and during a conference she didn't hesitate to castigate the President. 'I don't think President Bush is doing anything at all about AIDS,' she said. 'I'm not sure he even knows how to spell "AIDS".' Once again she embarked on a huge enterprise: to find the means to finance AIDS research and to combat homophobic prejudice: 'AIDS is not a sin. It's a disease, a virus. How dare these so-called religious people use this illness to discriminate against homosexuals?' Defending the homosexual community, she added, 'I know so many homosexuals. There would be no art in America if it weren't for gays!'

Elizabeth was approaching 55 when she launched her perfume 'Elizabeth Taylor's Passion' in early 1987. This luxury product soon brought her a fortune, becoming the fourth most popular women's fragrance sold in the US and making her one of the richest women in the country – her net worth was reported to be $80 million. A second fragrance, 'White Diamonds' was launched a few years later followed by 'Black Pearls', and it is estimated that yearly sales of these three perfumes total $200 million.

The entrepreneurial actress decided to embark on another profitable project: a book telling the story of her fight against alcohol and her struggles to lose weight. *Elizabeth Takes Off* was phenomenally successful. An accomplished businesswoman, Elizabeth travelled round the world promoting it, but when she returned to Los Angeles in July 1988 the drinking and overeating began again. She also began to suffer from osteoporosis and the vicious cycle quickly resumed as she swallowed every painkiller she could get her hands on. On 25 October she returned to the Betty Ford Center, where she remained for another seven interminable weeks detoxing but regaining all the weight she had just lost.

A 37-year-old man named Larry Fortensky was also undergoing detoxification at the Betty Ford Center. Twenty years her junior, this truck driver and construction worker had little in common with the Hollywood diva. Doubtless this is what attracted Elizabeth, who felt she could erase the past and make a new beginning with him. For her handsome new lover, she decided to embark on a draconian diet, dropping from 82 to 54 kilos (180lbs to 119lbs) in several weeks.

Was she once again acting out a scene from her own life when she decided to take the part of Alexandra del Lago, an ageing, drug- and alcohol-addicted movie queen with a much younger lover? Whatever the case, the role suited her perfectly and *Sweet Bird of Youth*, a made-for-television movie from Tennessee Williams's play, was undoubtedly Elizabeth's best work for many years.

Just before she turned 58, she was urgently hospitalized in Santa Monica. As in 1961, serious pneumonia was diagnosed and once again she was close to death. In October 1991 Elizabeth and Larry married in an extravagant ceremony at her friend Michael Jackson's famous Neverland ranch. The flamboyant wedding cost $1.5 million, with $125,000 spent on flowers. As a dedicated businesswoman, Elizabeth took advantage of the occasion to promote her second fragrance 'White Diamonds', the scent of which she humorously described as 'evocative of a torrid fling at sunset'.

The newlyweds honeymooned in Europe before celebrating Elizabeth's 60th birthday at Disneyland, hired for the evening. 'I can't get over turning 60', she exulted. In a spirit of self-mockery, she agreed to do a voiceover for *The Simpsons* and made a hilarious appearance in *The Flintstones*.

The Queen of Hollywood becomes a goddess

In 1993, the American Film Institute decided to honour Elizabeth Taylor with their Lifetime Achievement Award. After a 50-year career, the actress had become a living symbol of the great age of American cinema.

But when Larry decided to quit his construction work he started drinking again. The unlikely fairytale between the fabulously wealthy actress and the poor blue-collar worker had lasted longer than anyone expected and it was not until February 1996 that the couple announced that they had started divorce proceedings.

Elizabeth learned of the death of her mother Sara, whom she had installed in a luxury condominium in Palm Springs. Although her death was not unexpected, Elizabeth felt a great sense of loss. Alone in her large house, in pain following two hip operations, she once again turned to alcohol and medication.

For two years after her separation from Larry, Elizabeth lived in seclusion. In February 1997 she suddenly began having spells of memory loss; tests were made and it was discovered that she had a brain tumour. Always courageous when confronted with illness or adversity, she underwent an operation and the woman who had faced her own mortality many times pulled through once again. Even she could hardly believe it, as she declared after this 75th surgical intervention: 'I feel reborn. I want to give back the love that I've been given.'

In 1999 she had a fall and was in a wheelchair when she visited Buckingham Palace in May 2000 to be invested as a Dame Commander of the Order of the British Empire by Queen Elizabeth. She made her last screen appearance in 2001 in *These Old Broads,* a hilarious made-for-television movie produced by ABC in which she played the manager of three ageing actresses trying to make a comeback, alongside Shirley MacLaine, Debbie Reynolds and Joan Collins.

She blossomed, resumed giving dinner parties, began to go out again and was eager to meet people; at the age of 69 she re-embraced life. And in 2001 she published her second book, *My Love Affair with Jewelry*, about her passion for gems. Continuing her savvy business acumen, she also brought out a line of luxury wigs that would earn her another small fortune. In the meantime she fell in love, first with Rod Steiger, then with her dentist. However in 2002 her health deteriorated and she suffered tachycardia and osteoporosis; she declared with typical humour, 'I've been pronounced dead; I didn't breathe, I went through the tunnel with the white light and the rest of it. I've almost died several times. I really dreaded waking up to find myself alive every morning.' She affirmed that she had not taken a drop of alcohol for some 15 years. In 2003, during the Oscar ceremonies, she made her formal farewell to the big screen, repeating it on television: 'This will be my swansong. I'm retiring from the business; it doesn't interest me any longer. I find it superficial because my life is now dedicated to AIDS, not to acting.'

She revealed to the press that she had decided to donate her wealth to the struggle against AIDS, saying 'I want to leave the bulk of my fortune to the American Foundation for Aids Reseach, which I set up in 1985 following the death of my great friend Rock Hudson. The fight against this scourge has become my life's struggle. My children are all doing well, with pleasant houses, and I have always been generous to them. They will have to settle for mementoes.'

At 76, Elizabeth still lives in her Bel Air house, transformed into a kind of museum dedicated to her glory years. Surrounded by her photographs and masterpieces (including paintings by Monet, Renoir and the famous Andy Warhol portrait of her), her 18th-century furniture and her pets, she watches her films in her big projection room and at 4pm precisely is served English tea. Plump, fabulously wealthy (her fortune is estimated to be $150 million), she is incontestably the last survivor of Hollywood's golden age.

The woman now called 'the diva', 'the goddess' or even the 'sacred monster' of cinema's Mecca has survived 35 years of alcohol- and drug-dependence, a daily pack of cigarettes, the death of a husband, at least one suicide attempt and dozens of operations. With typical wry humour she gives her miracle-recipe for facing up to 'life's monstrosity': to love 'life, love and men'. Here is what seems to epitomize this outstanding woman. The life of the violet-eyed actress has not been a model of wisdom or virtue but as she so rightly said, 'the problem with people who have no vices is that you can be almost positive that they'll have boring virtues.' There's no doubt that the life of Elizabeth Taylor – with its excesses, drunkenness, bliss and affliction, egotism and altruism – has been anything but boring.

"I never wanted to be an actress, it was forced on me."

Elizabeth Taylor

1934 / Elizabeth Taylor aged two.

1934 / Elizabeth Taylor aged two, with her mother Sara and her brother Howard.

1935 / Elizabeth Taylor at three.

1934 / Elizabeth Taylor aged two.

1936 / Elizabeth Taylor, four, and her brother Howard, aged seven.

1936/ Four-year-old Elizabeth Taylor on her pony Daisy.

1940/ Elizabeth Taylor aged seven, with her mother Sara and her brother Howard.

1942 / Aged ten, Elizabeth Taylor poses for her first portrait as an actress. She had a small part in *There's One Born Every Minute*, directed by Harold Young.

1944/ Elizabeth Taylor aged 12.

1946/ Elizabeth Taylor, 14, reads a comic in her bedroom.

1948/ Elizabeth Taylor, 16, and her friend Roddy McDowall play on the beach.

1946/ Elizabeth Taylor, 14, and her brother Howard, 17, in front of the family home with their dog and cats.

1947/ At 15, Elizabeth Taylor took a screen-test for the film *Cynthia*, in which she starred the same year, directed by Robert Leonard.

1947/ Elizabeth Taylor at 15, when she played the title role in Robert Leonard's *Cynthia*. She received her first screen kiss in this film.

1948/ The 16-year-old Elizabeth Taylor poses with her cat.

1944/ Elizabeth Taylor in *National Velvet*, directed by Clarence Brown. The film earned five Oscar nominations and won two, including Best Supporting Actress for Anne Revere.

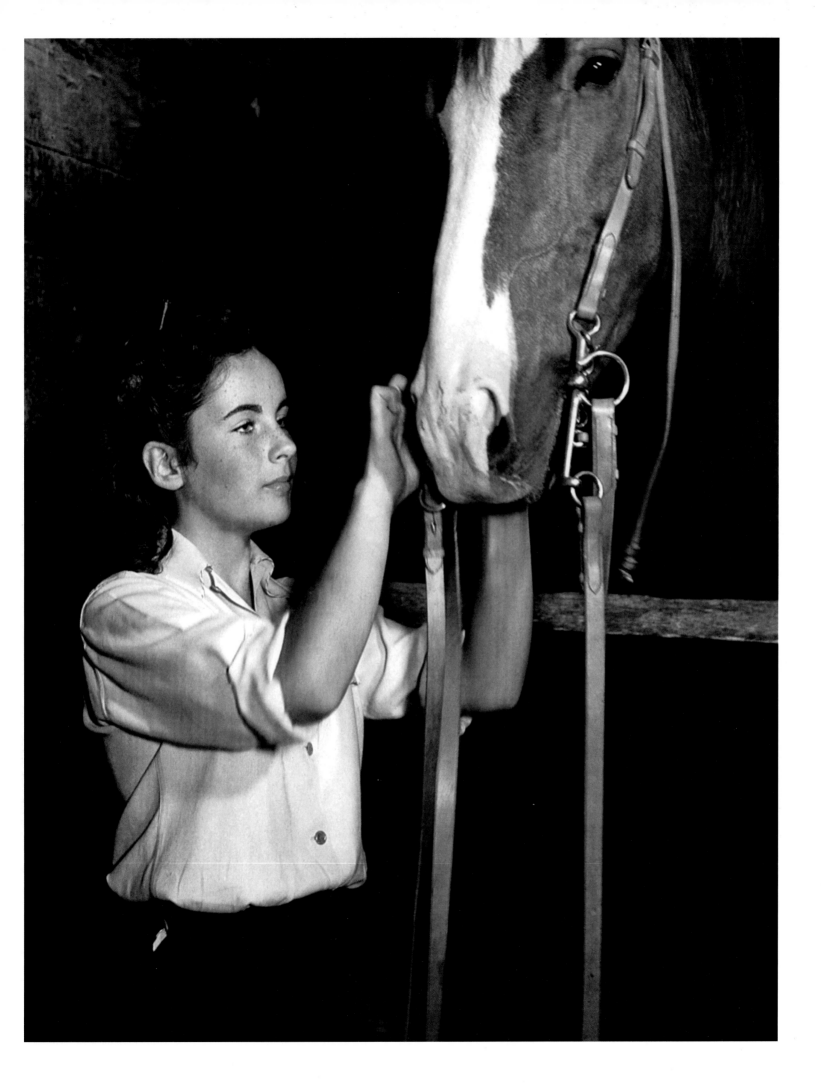

1949/ Elizabeth Taylor at 17,
while filming *Little Women*,
directed by Mervyn LeRoy.

1949/ In Mervyn LeRoy's *Little Women*, Elizabeth Taylor co-starred with Janet Leigh, June Allyson, Margaret O'Brien and Mary Astor.

1950/ Elizabeth Taylor wore the traditional gown for her diploma ceremony at the University of Los Angeles. She was accompanied by her mother, Sara.

1950/ Official portrait of the young graduate.

39

"I stopped being a child the minute I started working in pictures."

Elizabeth Taylor

1948/ Elizabeth Taylor poses for the cover of *Life* magazine.

1950/ Elizabeth Taylor and her first husband, Conrad Nicholson ('Nicky') Hilton Jr., on their wedding day, 6 May 1950.

1950/ Nicky Hilton and Elizabeth Taylor cut their wedding cake.

1950/ Elizabeth Taylor, aged 18.

1951/ Elizabeth Taylor in *A Place in the Sun*, directed by George Stevens. The film won six Oscars and a Golden Globe Award for Best Film.

1952/ Elizabeth Taylor at 20, during filming of *Love is Better than Ever*, directed by Stanley Donen. In her private life, however, love did not last: when filming ended the actress divorced her first husband, Nicky Hilton, heir to the hotel empire.

1951/ Elizabeth Taylor at 19 during filming of *A Place in the Sun*, directed by George Stevens and adapted from Theodore Dreiser's novel, *An American Tragedy*. She co-starred with Montgomery Clift, who remained a close friend until his sudden death in 1966.

1952 / *Ivanhoe*, directed by
Richard Thorpe, would be
nominated in the Best Film
category at the Oscars and
Golden Globe Awards, and was
a big commercial success.

1952 / Elizabeth Taylor at 20
during the filming of *Ivanhoe*.
For the first time in her career,
her mother was absent from
the film set.

"If you hear me talking about marriage, slap me!"

Elizabeth Taylor

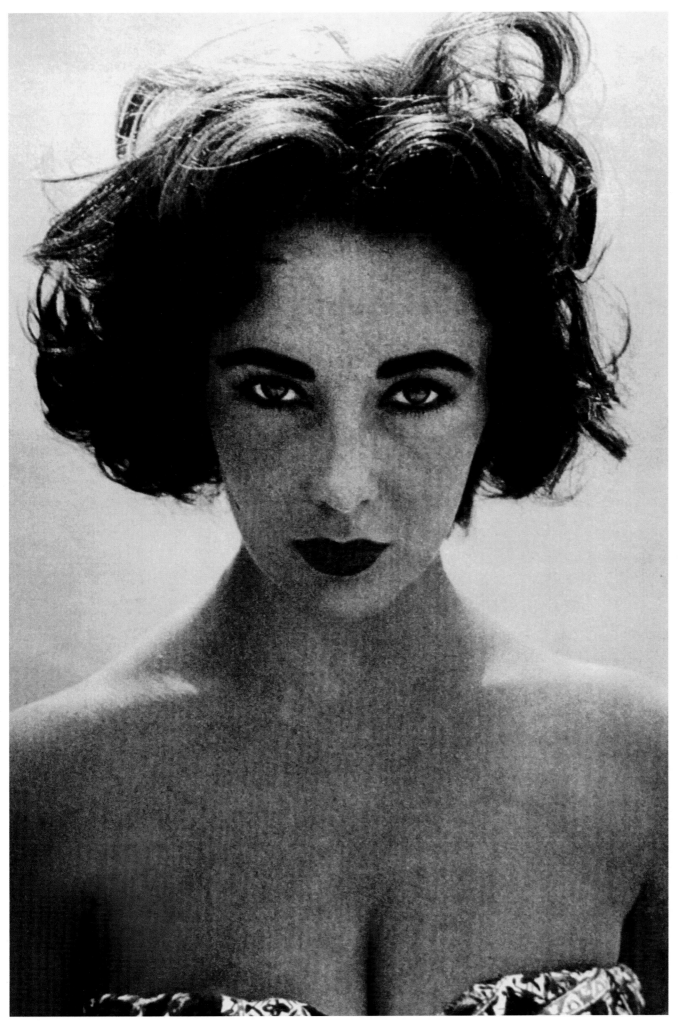

1956 / Elizabeth Taylor, aged 24.

1954/ Elizabeth poses with her son, Michael Howard Wilding, for the August number of *Look* magazine. The issue was devoted to 'Hollywood mothers'.

1955/ Michael Wilding, Elizabeth Taylor's second husband, amuses himself by feeding their son, Michael Wilding Jr., aged two.

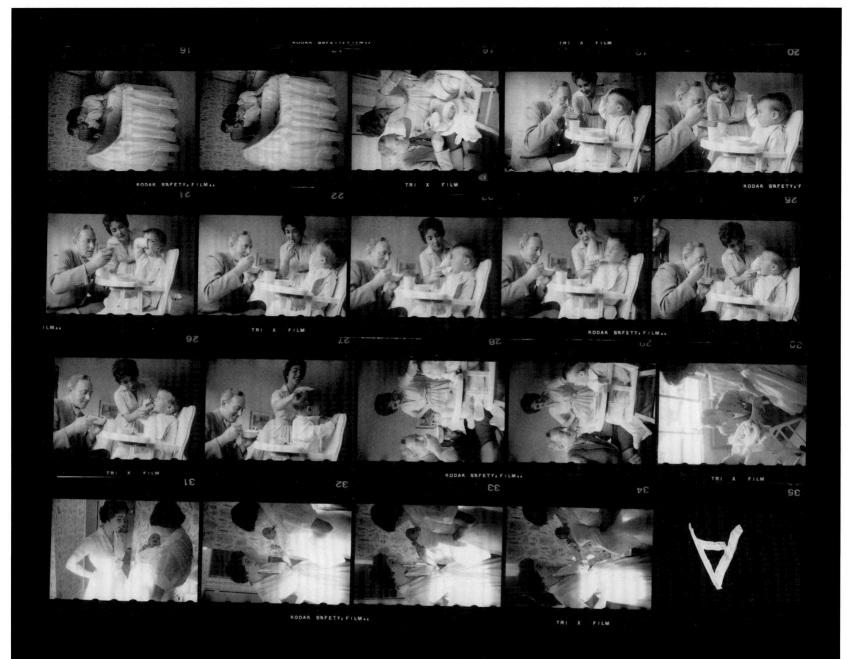

1956 / Poster for *Giant*, directed by George Stevens. The film earned five Oscar nominations and won the Best Director Award.

1955 / Elizabeth Taylor and James Dean developed a special relationship during the filming of *Giant*. Here, Dean fools around between takes by pretending to strangle his co-star.

Previous pages :
1956/ A lunch-break on the set of *Giant*, directed by George Stevens.

1955/ James Dean welcomes Elizabeth Taylor and Pat Westmore to his trailer during the filming of *Giant*.

1955 / The actors leave the set at Marfa, Texas, to spend the weekend in Dallas.

"I feel very adventurous. There are so many doors to be opened, and I'm not afraid to look behind them."

Elizabeth Taylor

1955 / Elizabeth Taylor aged
23, in Texas during the filming
of *Giant*.

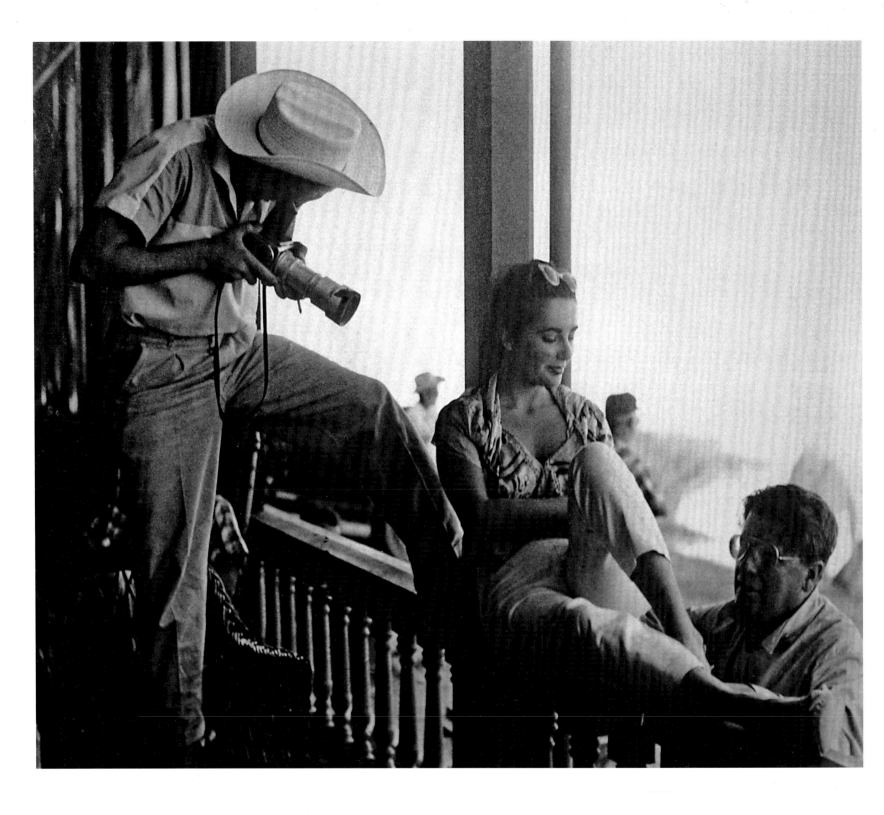

Previous pages :
1955/ James Dean leafs through a copy of *Look* magazine, featuring Elizabeth Taylor, who is asleep beside him, on the cover.

1956/ While on the set of *Giant*, James Dean borrowed Sid Avery's camera to take a photograph of Elizabeth Taylor, which he discusses here with the director George Stevens.
1956/ Elizabeth Taylor sunbathes during the filming of *Giant* in Texas.
66

"I had an acting lesson and didn't know how to act *per se*. I just developed as an actress. Acting is instinctive with me."

Elizabeth Taylor

1957/ A picture taken on the set of *Raintree Country*, directed by Edward Dmytryk.

1956 / Elizabeth Taylor and her husband Michael Wilding, both fans of bullfighting, play-act a corrida in the garden of their Hollywood house.

1957 / For her part in *Raintree Country*, Elizabeth Taylor had to wear a corset that she found very uncomfortable, but she threw herself into the role of a Southern belle not unlike Scarlett O'Hara.

1957 / In Edward Dmytryk's *Raintree Country*, Elizabeth Taylor was reunited with her friend Montgomery Clift.

1957 / Her interpretation of Susanna Drake in *Raintree Country* earned Elizabeth Taylor another Academy Award nomination. The film was also nominated for Best Costume Design, Music and Art Direction.

"I don't pretend to be an ordinary housewife."

Elizabeth Taylor

1956 / Elizabeth Taylor holds her second child, Christopher. Barely one year old, he shares a birthday with his mother — 27 February.

78

1957/ Elizabeth Taylor gives a bottle to her daughter Liza, watched attentively by her two sons, Michael and Christopher, and her husband, Mike Todd.

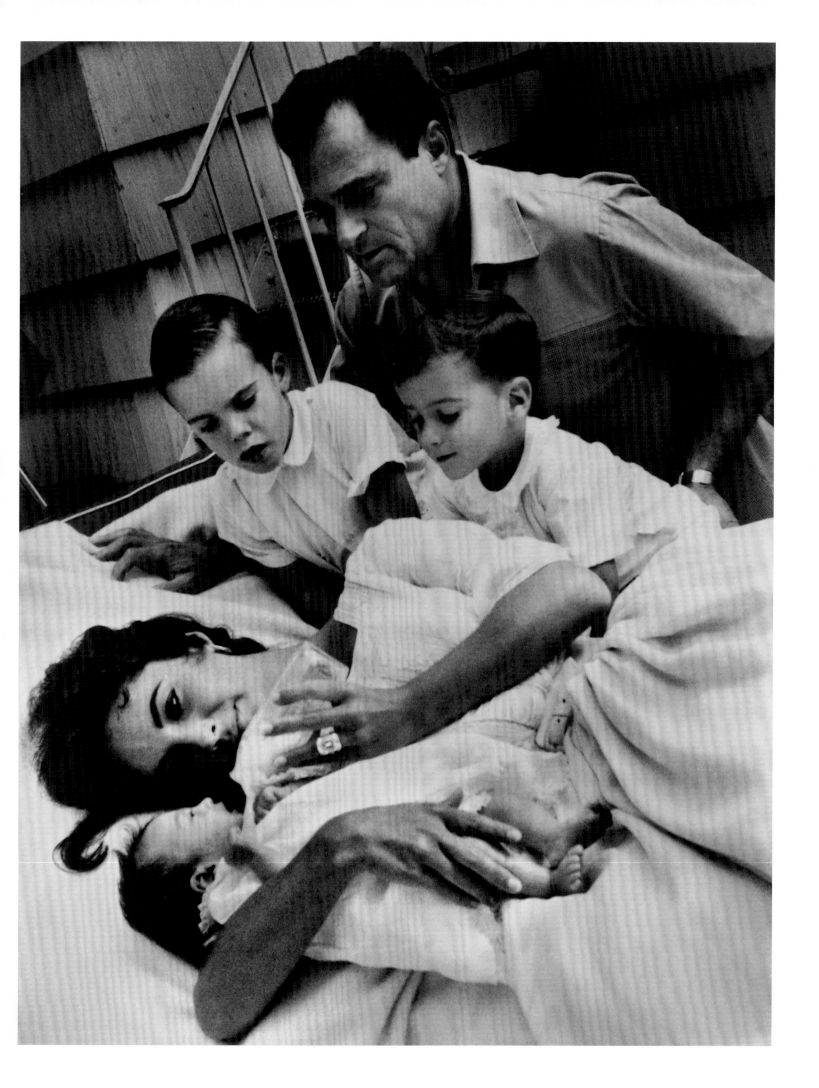

Previous pages :
1957 / Elizabeth Taylor and her husband Mike Todd.

1957 / Elizabeth Taylor holds her newborn daughter Elizabeth Frances, nicknamed 'Liza'. It was the actress's third child and the only one she had with her third husband, Mike Todd, who would die a year later in an airplane accident.

1955/ Elizabeth Taylor plays with her children, Michael and Christopher.

"I had the body of a woman and the emotions of a child."

Elizabeth Taylor

Previous spread :
1958 / A family portrait taken at home: Mike Todd, Elizabeth Taylor and their sons Michael and Christopher.

88

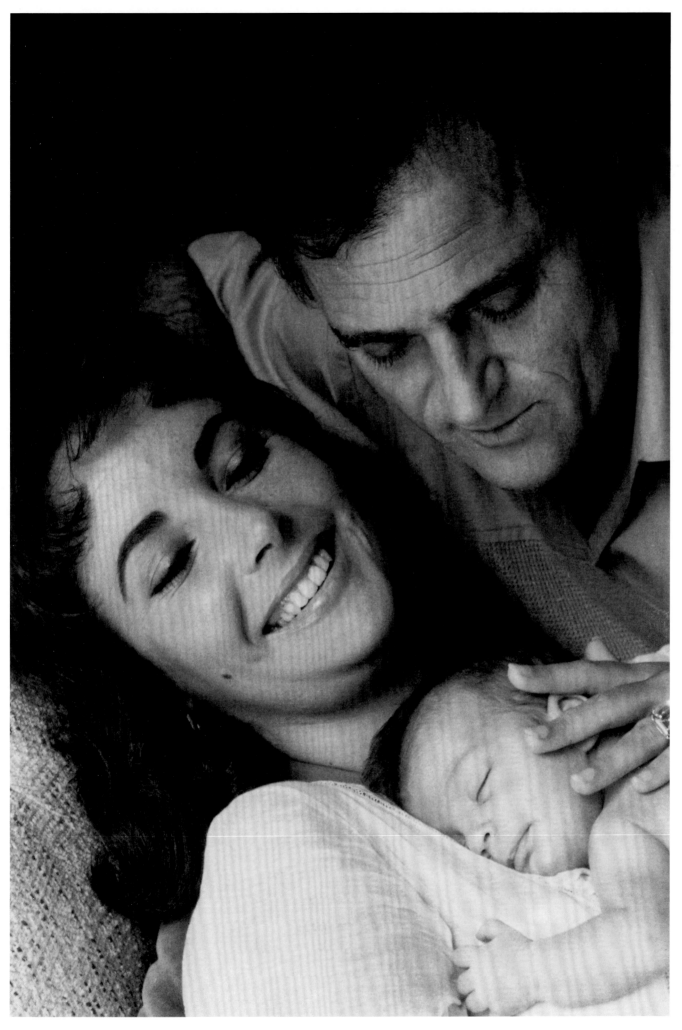

1957/ On 6 August, Elizabeth gave birth to a third child, Elizabeth Frances, always known as 'Liza'.

1958 / Elizabeth Taylor with daughter Liza on her knee, and her sons Michael and Christopher.

1958 / A family weekend for Elizabeth Taylor, her husband Mike Todd, and her two sons, Michael and Christopher.

1959 / Elizabeth Taylor and her son Christopher Wilding Jr.

1965 / Howard Taylor (Elizabeth's brother) pictured on his boat with his wife, his children, Elizabeth, her husband Richard Burton, and her children by her second husband, Michael Wilding, Michael Jr. and Christopher.

"Marriage is like a meal in a restaurant: you have to digest it before you know if you've made the right choice."

Elizabeth Taylor

1959/ Elizabeth Taylor leaves the Dorchester Hotel, London.

1957/ En route to the location shooting of *Raintree Country* in Danville, Kentucky: Elizabeth Taylor sleeps beside Marguerite Lamkin, her dialogue coach.

1958 / Elizabeth Taylor and Paul Newman shared billing for *Cat on a Hot Tin Roof*, directed by Richard Brooks. The film was adapted from Tennessee Williams' Pulitzer Prize-winning play.

1958 / *Cat on a Hot Tin Roof*, starring Elizabeth Taylor and Paul Newman, was nominated for six Academy Awards, notably for Best Actor, Best Actress and Best Director.

"The problem with people who have no vices is that you can be practically sure they're going to have some pretty annoying virtues."

Elizabeth Taylor

Previous pages :
1959 / Filming *Suddenly, Last Summer,* for which the screenplay was written by Tennessee Williams and Gore Vidal.

102

1959/ Elizabeth Taylor on the set of *Suddenly, Last Summer*, directed by Joseph L. Mankiewicz. She described this film as 'the most emotionally draining' but also 'the most emotionally stimulating' professional experience of her life.

Previous pages :
1959/ Her performance in *Suddenly, Last Summer* earned Elizabeth Taylor her third Academy Award nomination for Best Actress but she failed to win the coveted Oscar.

1959/ Elizabeth Taylor and her son Christopher in S'Agaro, Spain.

106

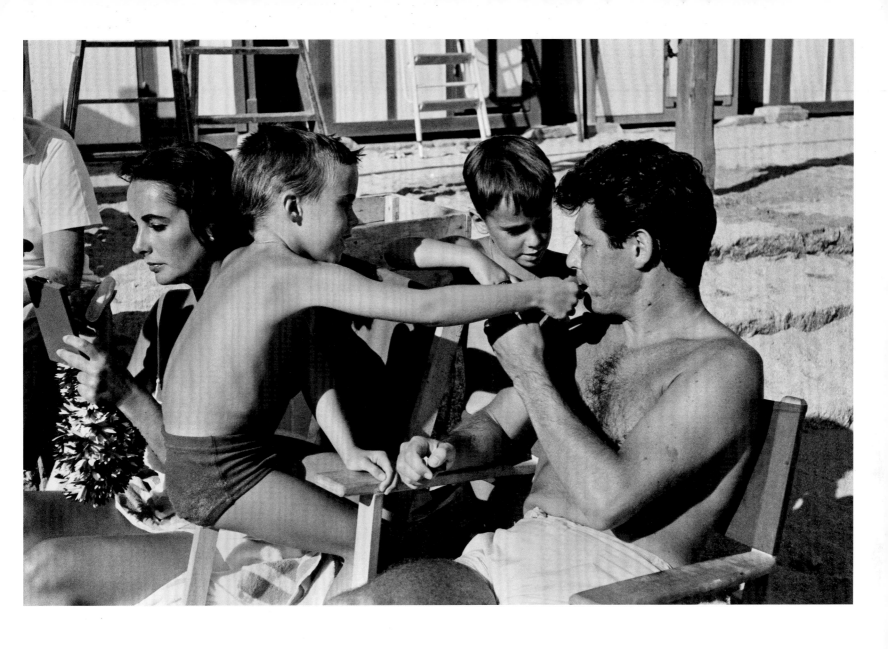

1959/ Taking a break from filming *Suddenly, Last Summer,* Elizabeth Taylor relaxes on a family holiday in Spain, with her sons Christopher and Michael and her husband Eddie Fisher.

1959 / Elizabeth Taylor and her
sons Christopher and Michael in
S'Agaro, Spain.

1959/ Elizabeth Taylor, her fourth husband, Eddie Fisher, and her son Christopher by her second husband, Michael Wilding.

"If someone's dumb enough to offer me a million dollars to make a picture, I'm certainly not dumb enough to turn it down."

Elizabeth Taylor

1959/Elizabeth Taylor at 27.

1959/ Elizabeth Taylor on the set of *Suddenly, Last Summer,* directed by Joseph L. Mankiewicz. She co-starred with Katharine Hepburn and Montgomery Clift. This was the first film she made after the death of her third husband, Mike Todd, in an airplane accident.

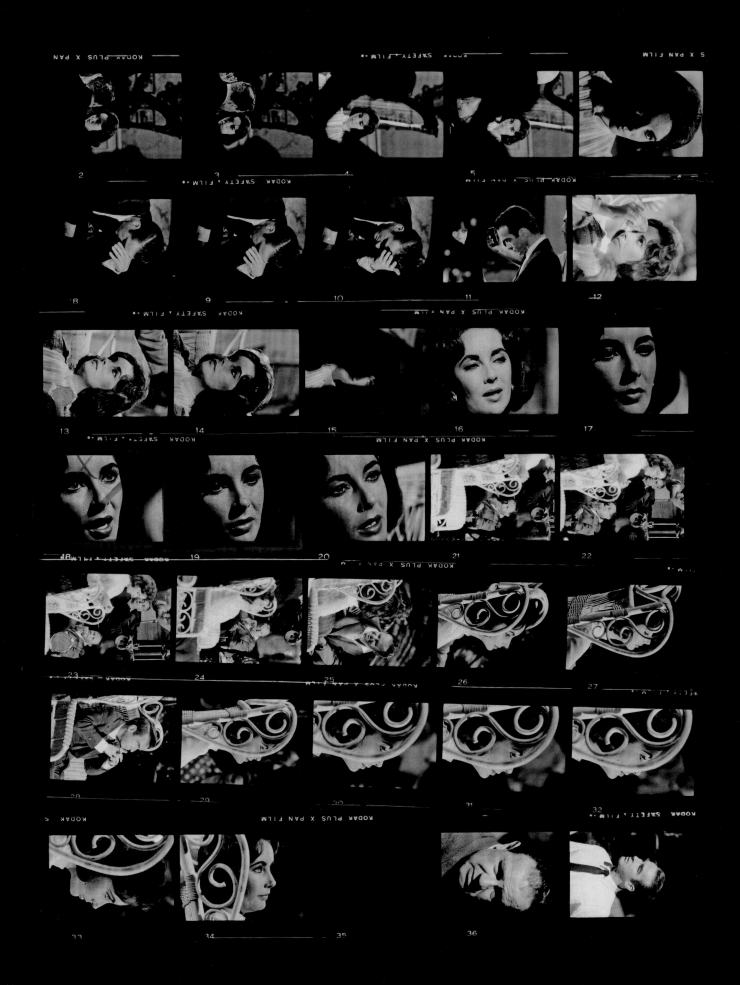

1959/ Elizabeth Taylor and Montgomery Clift wait in their dressing-rooms during a break in filming.

"You find out who your real friends are when you're involved in a scandal."

Elizabeth Taylor

Previous pages :
1959 / Elizabeth Taylor in London while filming *Suddenly, Last Summer*, directed by Joseph L. Mankiewicz.

1960 / Elizabeth Taylor aged 28.

120

1960 / Poster for *Butterfield 8*, directed by Daniel Mann.

1960/ MGM exploited Elizabeth Taylor's scandalous image by casting her as a high-class call-girl in *Butterfield 8*. The actress detested the part, but she won her first Oscar for it, after three nominations.

Elizabeth Taylor

1956 / To mark the premiere of *Giant*, Elizabeth Taylor leaves her handprints on the celebrated Walk of Fame at Grauman's Chinese Theatre, Hollywood. Behind her is Rock Hudson with director George Stevens alongside.

1961 / Elizabeth Taylor won the Best Actress Oscar for her role in *Butterfield 8*, directed by Daniel Mann.

1968 / Elizabeth Taylor and Maria Callas at the premiere of the play *La Puce a l'Oreille (A Flea in her Ear)* at the Marigny Theatre, Paris. Richard Burton is behind them and Baron Guy de Rothschild and his second wife, Baroness Marie-Hélène de Rothschild, are in front.

1967 / Elizabeth Taylor and Aristotle Onassis at a masked ball in Palazzo Rezzonico, organized in aid of Venice's flood victims.

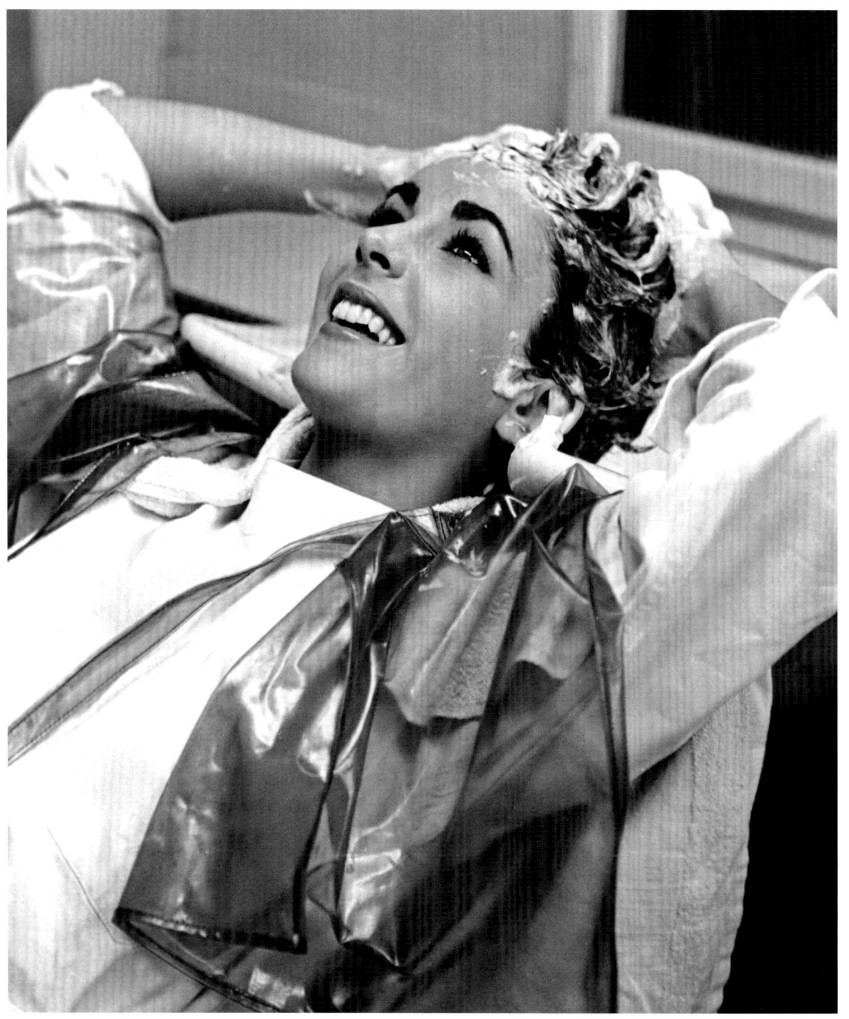

1952 / Elizabeth Taylor in her dressing-room during filming of *Ivanhoe*, directed by Richard Thorpe.

1963 / Elizabeth Taylor touches up her makeup on set while filming *Cleopatra*.

"I've been through it all, baby, I'm Mother Courage."

Elizabeth Taylor

1963 / Elizabeth Taylor poses in her dressing-room during the filming of *The VIPs*. In Anthony Asquith's film, she co-starred with her husband, Richard Burton, and with Margaret Rutherford, who won an Academy Award for Best Supporting Actress.

130

1963 / Poster for *Cleopatra*, directed by Joseph Mankiewicz, with Richard Burton, Elizabeth Taylor and Rex Harrison. The film won seven awards, including four Oscars.

1963 / Elizabeth Taylor aged 31, while filming the mythical role of *Cleopatra*.

1963 / A powerful woman, Elizabeth Taylor fought with the studios and negotiated the best contract in cinema history for the role of Cleopatra.

1963 / Elizabeth Taylor prepares for a gala evening under the attentive gaze of her future husband, Richard Burton.

"Life isn't just about money…it's also about furs and jewellery."

Elizabeth Taylor

1973 / A portrait taken during the filming of Larry Peerce's *Ash Wednesday*; Elizabeth was then 41.

140

1963 / Elizabeth Taylor and Richard Burton, always very cosy together.

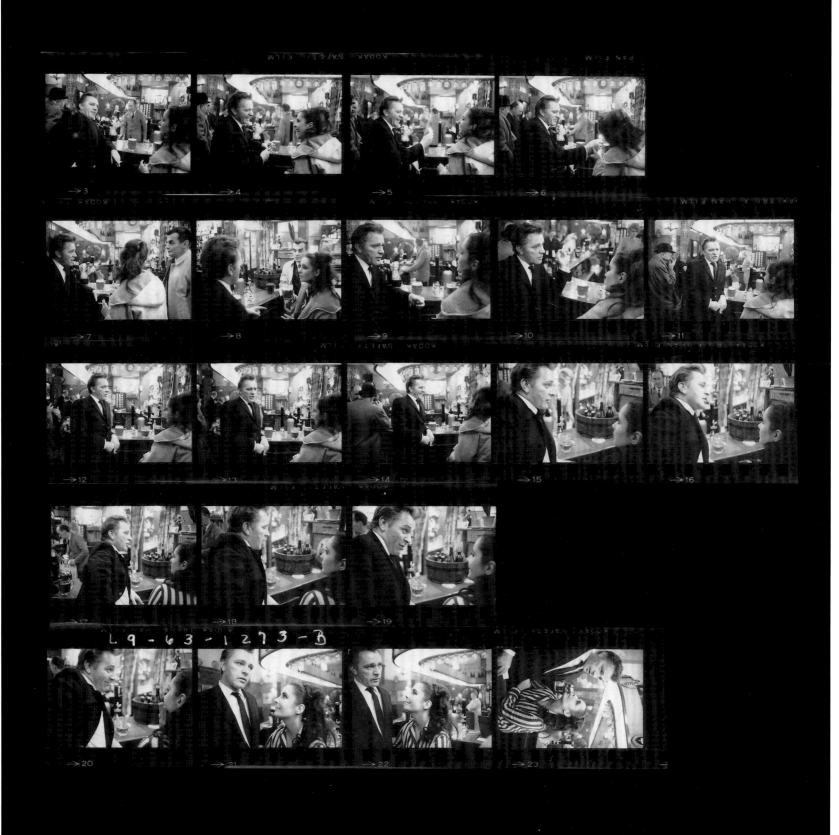

1963 / Elizabeth Taylor and her future husband, Richard Burton, have a drink at the bar of their hotel.

1964 / Elizabeth Taylor marries Richard Burton.

1968 / Elizabeth Taylor and her husband, Richard Burton, at Bristol television studios. Elizabeth is wearing the ring with the 33.19-carat Krupp diamond (formerly owned by Vera Krupp), which they bought at auction.

"I'm infatuated with being in love."

Elizabeth Taylor

1965 / Richard Burton and Elizabeth Taylor, one year after their first wedding.

148

1964 / Richard Burton and Elizabeth Taylor: one of Hollywood's iconic couples.

1964 / Elizabeth Taylor and her daughter Liza on the cover of *Look* magazine.

LOOK

NOW MORE THAN 7,400,000 CIRCULATION

25 CENTS · APRIL 21, 1964

GOLD-WATER SPEAKS

STAN MUSIAL'S OWN STORY

ELIZABETH TAYLOR AND HER DAUGHTER

1964 / At Puerta Vallarta, Mexico, Elizabeth Taylor relaxes between two films in the house given to her by her future husband, Richard Burton.

1966 / Elizabeth Taylor and Richard Burton reading the script on the set of *Who's Afraid of Virginia Woolf?*

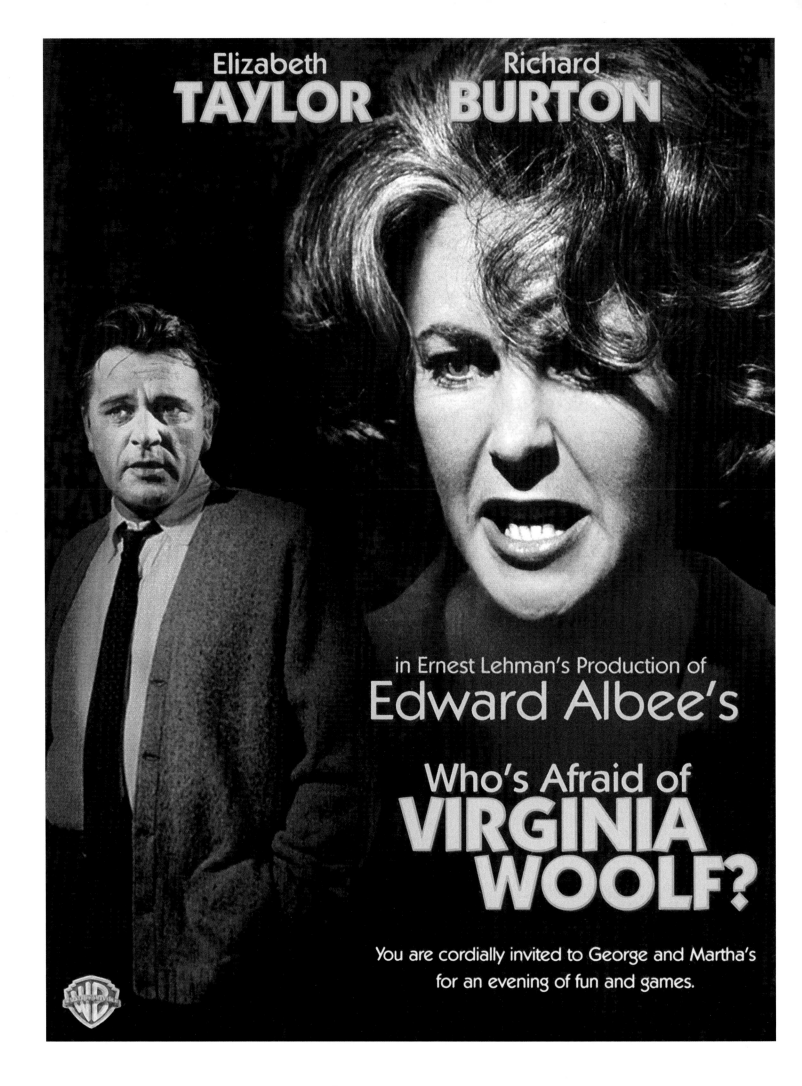

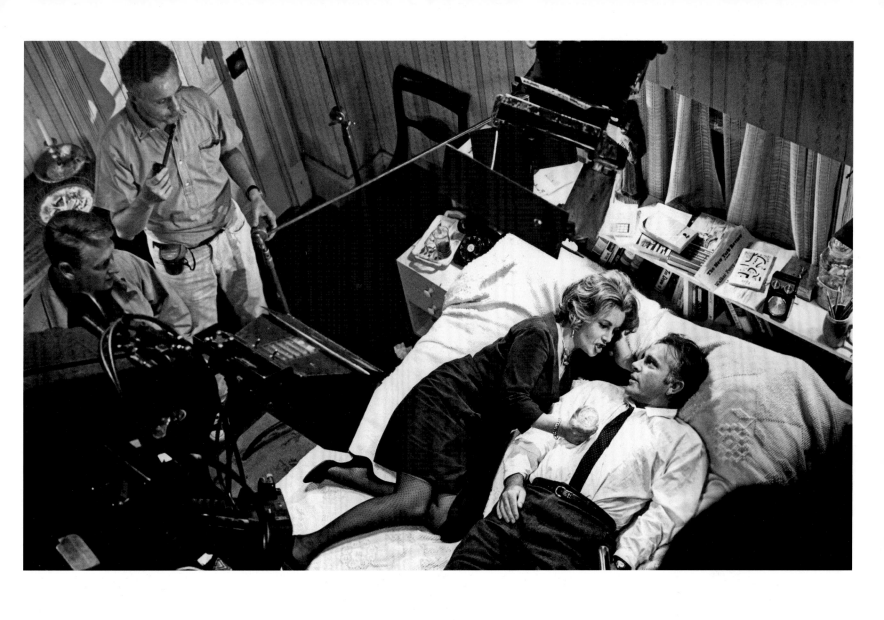

1966 / Poster for the film *Who's Afraid of Virginia Woolf?*, directed by Mike Nichols. The film would win 18 awards, including five Oscars.

1966 / Mike Nichols directs a scene during filming of *Who's Afraid of Virginia Woolf?* To play the part of Martha, Elizabeth Taylor had to gain weight, change her voice and age 20 years with makeup. Her performance won her a second Best Actress Oscar.

"Success is a great deodorant. It takes away all the old smells."

Elizabeth Taylor

1970 / Elizabeth Taylor seated next to her husband Richard Burton at a dinner following the 42nd Oscars ceremony.

1963 / Richard Burton and Elizabeth Taylor in their dressing-room at Elstree Studios, near London, where they were filming *The VIPs*, directed by Anthony Asquith.

1963 / Elizabeth Taylor plays with her dog, which she took almost everywhere.

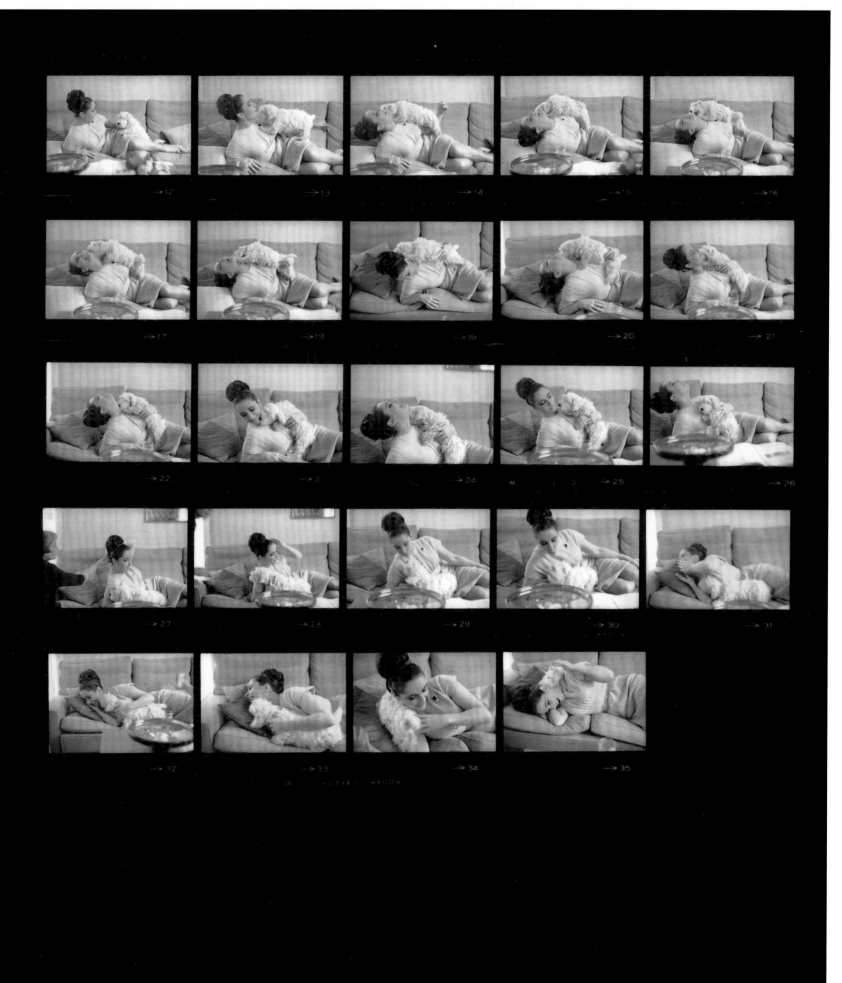

"Marriage is a rest period between two passions."

Elizabeth Taylor

1963 / Elizabeth Taylor, aged 31,
and Richard Burton.

1968 / Elizabeth Taylor attends a dinner organized by supporters of Robert Kennedy, in the presence of his wife Ethel. The White House candidate would be assassinated several months later.

1972 / Elizabeth Taylor in London.

1976 / Elizabeth Taylor meets HRH Queen Elizabeth II, who would make her a Dame of the British Empire 23 years later.

1965 / Elizabeth Taylor on the set of *The Sandpiper*, directed by Vincente Minnelli, for which she pocketed a fee of $1 million.

1965 / Elizabeth Taylor aged 33.

1965 / Elizabeth Taylor got to know Ernest Lehman during the filming of *The Sandpiper*. He suggested that she should star in his latest project, the film adaptation of a play he had just seen and adored: *Who's Afraid of Virginia Woolf?*

1965 / Elizabeth Taylor in Vincente Minnelli's *The Sandpiper*. The film music won an Oscar, a Golden Globe and a Grammy Award.

"I'm a survivor – a living example of what people can go through and survive."

Elizabeth Taylor

1968/ Elizabeth Taylor on the set of *Boom!* Tennessee Williams wrote the screenplay for Joseph Losey's film.

1968 / Richard Burton helps Elizabeth Taylor to adjust the hood of her costume during the filming of Joseph Losey's *Boom!*

1968 / Elizabeth Taylor and Richard Burton play dominoes in their dressing-room between takes while filming *Boom!* in Sardinia

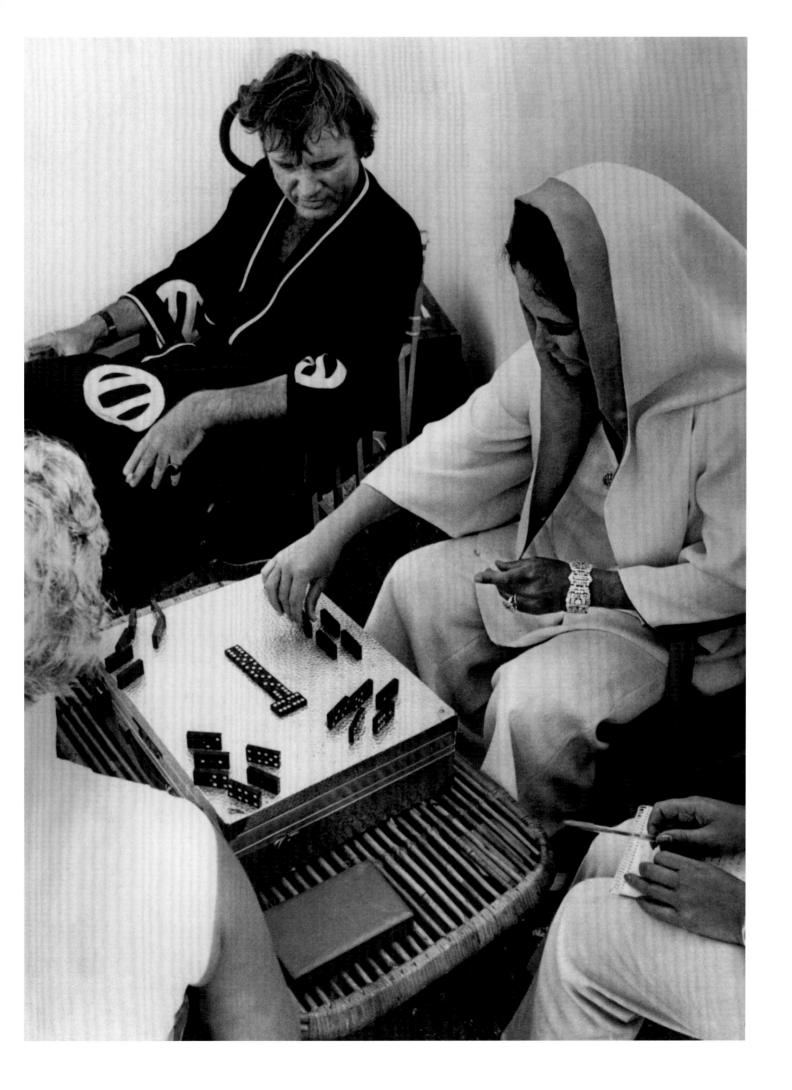

Quand 2 monstres sacrés jouent aux amants terribles

20th.CENTURY-FOX présente

Elizabeth Taylor / Warren Beatty

dans

Une Production George Stevens - Fred Kohlmar

Las Vegas... Un Couple

(The Only Game In Town)

Produit par FRED KOHLMAR • Réalisé par GEORGE STEVENS
Scénario de FRANK D. GILROY Tiré de sa pièce • Couleurs par DE LUXE®
VISA DE CENSURE N° 3647

1970 / Poster for *The Only Game in Town*, directed by George Stevens.

1970 / Warren Beatty's reputation as a womanizer was so great that Richard Burton paid frequent visits to his wife during filming of *The Only Game in Town*.

1970 / Frank Sinatra was originally cast in the role of Joe Grady in *The Only Game in Town*. But filming delays meant that it was Warren Beatty who finally co-starred with Elizabeth Taylor.

1970 / Although the action of *The Only Game in Town* was supposed take place in the US, all the interior scenes were filmed in Paris, since the contracts of Richard Burton and Elizabeth Taylor stipulated that they must never be more than one hour apart.

"Acting is, to me now, artificial. Seeing people suffer is real. It couldn't be more real."

Elizabeth Taylor

1970 / Elizabeth Taylor attends the 7th annual Publicists Guild Awards in Los Angeles.

1977 / Elizabeth Taylor marries John Warner, whom she supported during his successful campaign for election as a senator for Virginia.

1991/ With tremendous publicity, Elizabeth Taylor launches a range of perfumes in the US.

1975/ Elizabeth Taylor one year after her second divorce from Richard Burton.

"I want to leave the bulk of my fortune to the American Foundation for Aids Research, which I created in 1985 (...). The fight against this scourge has become my life's struggle."

Elizabeth Taylor

1985 / Elizabeth Taylor receives the Cross of a Commander of Arts and Letters in Paris.

Filmography

1942	*There's One Born Every Minute* directed by Harold Young
1943	*Lassie Come Home* directed by Fred M. Wilcox
1944	*Jane Eyre* directed by Robert Stevenson
1944	*The White Cliffs of Dover* directed by Clarence Brown
1944	*National Velvet* directed by Clarence Brown
1946	*Courage of Lassie* directed by Fred M. Wilcox
1947	*Life with Father* directed by Michael Curtiz
1947	*Cynthia* directed by Robert Z. Leonard
1948	*A Date with Judy* by Richard Thorpe
1948	*Julia Misbehaves* by Jack Conway
1949	*Little Women* directed by Mervyn LeRoy
1949	*Conspirator* directed by Victor Saville
1950	*The Big Hangover* directed by Norman Krasna
1950	*Father of the Bride* directed by Vincente Minnelli
1951	*Father's Little Dividend* directed by Vincente Minnelli
1951	*A Place in the Sun* directed by George Stevens
1951	*Quo Vadis* directed by Mervyn LeRoy
1951	*Callaway went Thataway* directed by Norman Panama
1952	*Love Is Better Than Ever* directed by Stanley Donen
1952	*Ivanhoe* directed by Richard Thorpe
1953	*The Girl Who Had Everything* directed by Richard Thorpe
1954	*Rhapsody* directed by Charles Vidor
1954	*Elephant Walk* directed by William Dieterle
1954	*Beau Brummell* directed by Curtis Bernhardt
1954	*The Last Time I Saw Paris* directed by Richard Brooks
1956	*Giant* directed by George Stevens
1957	*Raintree County* directed by Edward Dmytryk
1958	*Cat on a Hot Tin Roof* directed by Richard Brooks
1959	*Suddenly, Last Summer* directed by Joseph L. Mankiewicz
1960	*The Scent of Mystery* directed by Jack Cardiff (uncredited role)
1960	*Butterfield 8* directed by Daniel Mann
1963	*Cleopatra* directed by Joseph L. Mankiewicz
1963	*The VIPs* directed by Anthony Asquith
1965	*The Sandpiper* directed by Vincente Minnelli
1966	*Who's Afraid of Virginia Woolf?* directed by Mike Nichols
1967	*The Taming of the Shrew* directed by Franco Zeffirelli
1967	*The Heart of Show Business* directed by Alan Tarrant & Dennis Vance
1967	*Doctor Faustus* directed by Richard Burton & Nevill Coghill
1967	*Reflections in a Golden Eye* directed by John Huston
1967	*The Comedians* directed by Peter Glenville
1968	*Boom!* directed by Joseph Losey
1968	Secret Ceremony directed by Joseph Losey
1969	*Anne of the Thousand Days* directed by (uncredited role)
1970	*The Only Game in Town* directed by George Stevens
1972	*Zee and Co.* (US title: *X, Y, and Zee*) directed by Brian G. Hutton
1972	*Under Milk Wood* directed by Andrew Sinclair
1972	*Hammersmith Is Out* directed by Peter Ustinov
1973	*Divorce His, Divorce Hers* directed by Waris Hussein (TV)
1973	*Night Watch* directed by Brian G. Hutton
1973	*Ash Wednesday* directed by Larry Peerce

1974   *Identikit* (US title: *The Driver's Seat*) directed by Giuseppe Patroni Griffi
1976   *The Blue Bird* directed by George Cukor
1976   *Victory at Entebbe* directed by Marvin J. Chomsky (TV)
1978   *A Little Night Music* directed by Harold Prince
1978   *Return Engagement* directed by Joseph Hardy (TV)
1979   *Winter Kills* directed by William Richert (uncredited role)
1980   *The Mirror Crack'd* directed by Guy Hamilton
1983   *Between Friends* directed by Lou Antonio (TV)
1984   *Hotel* directed by Vince McEveety
1985   *Malice in Wonderland* directed by Gus Trikonis (TV)
1985   *North and South* directed by Richard Heffron (TV)
1986   *There Must Be a Pony* directed by Joseph Sargent (TV)
1987   *Poker Alice* directed by Arthur Allan Seidelman (TV)
1988   *Giovane Toscanini, Il* (US title: *Young Toscanini*) directed by Franco Zeffirelli
1989   *Sweet Bird of Youth* directed by Nicolas Roeg (TV)
1994   *The Flintstones* directed by Brian Levant
2001   *These Old Broads* directed by Matthew Diamond (TV)

Important Dates

1932 – Born in London, 27 February.

1939 – On the outbreak of war her parents leave England and settle in California.

1940 – Makes her first film, *There's One Born Every Minute*, directed by Harold Young, and signs her first MGM contract for *Lassie Come Home*.

1944 – Her role in *National Velvet* propels her into the ranks of child stars; she is only 12.

1946 – Writes a children's book, *Nibbles and Me*. Her parents split up.

1947 – *Cynthia* confirms her status as a young star.

1949 – Makes the cover of *Time* magazine when *Little Women* opens.

1950 – Marries Nicky Hilton, heir to the hotel chain of the same name, whom she divorces a year later.

1951 – Hospitalized for depression. *A Place in the Sun* is a big success and wins six Oscars.

1952 – Marries the actor Michael Wilding.

1953 – Birth of her first son, Michael Howard Wilding.

1955 – Birth of her second son, Christopher, born on her birthday.

1957 – Divorces Michael Wilding and marries Mike Todd. Birth of her daughter Elizabeth Frances. Release of *Raintree Country*, which earns her a first Oscar nomination.

1958 – Death of her third husband, Mike Todd, in an aeroplane accident. *Cat on a Hot Tin Roof* released: her second Oscar nomination.

1959 – Marries singer Eddie Fisher. Her role in *Suddenly, Last Summer* earns her a third Oscar nomination and her first Golden Globe.

1961 – Wins her first Oscar for *Butterfield 8*. Starts filming *Cleopatra* and embarks on a romance with her co-star Richard Burton. Hospitalized, she comes close to death.

1963 – *Cleopatra* is panned by the critics but Elizabeth earns $7 million from the film.

1964 – Marries Richard Burton and publishes her autobiography, aged 32.

1966 – Release of *Who's Afraid of Virginia Woolf?*, for which she wins a second Oscar.

1974 – Divorces Richard Burton.

1975 – Elizabeth and Richard reconcile and re-marry.

1976 – Second divorce from Richard Burton.

1977 – Marries John Warner and actively supports his campaign for election to the US Senate from Virginia, which he wins.

1981 – Acts on Broadway in *The Little Foxes*. Divorces John Warner.

1983 – Co-stars on Broadway with Richard Burton in Noel Coward's *Private Lives*. Enters the Betty Ford Clinic for a detoxification cure.

1984 – Richard Burton dies in Switzerland. Elizabeth makes television movies.

1985 – Receives the Cecil B. DeMille Award at the Golden Globes.

1986 – Embarks on a 20-year campaign against AIDS. She testifies before Congress for an increase in federal funding for AIDS research.

1987 – Receives the French Légion d'honneur. Launches a range of perfumes.

1988 – Meets Larry Fortensky at the Betty Ford Clinic. Publishes a book on the secrets of her diet and well-being entitled *Elizabeth Takes Off*.

1991 – Marries Larry Fortensky.

1993 – Life Achievement Award from the American Film Institute.

1996 – Divorces Larry Fortensky.

1999 – Created Dame Commander of the British Empire by Queen Elizabeth II.

Acknowledgements

Noémie Couteau, Rodolphe de Pouzilhac, Arthur Lemaire Jr., Louis Marlin, ...this book is for you.

My thanks also go to:

Frédéric Brun, for his enthusiasm for fiery animated discussions, for the smoke of puros savoured with requisite slowness, and for his passion for all kinds of publishing. On to beautiful projects!

Matt Berman, who is much missed on the terraces of the Latin Quarter, and by all who loved hearing him laugh. Come back from New York soon!

Annie Goguelin, to whom I send strength to live this new stretch of life a little more peacefully.

Beverly W. Brannan, for her invaluable help with my picture research, her sparkling eye when she talks about photography and the unpublished and forgotten gems that she has allowed me to include in this work.

Yann-Brice Dherbier.

Credits